FRENCH VILLAGES

Suzanne Madon

Foreword
Denis Tillinac

MOLIÈRE

FOREWORD

For the most beautiful voyage in the world all you need is a car, a Michelin map and a taste for poetry. You can wander along our country roads through a thousand villages with a thousand different faces whose beauty is both glowing and secret.

When we discover Riquewihr among its vineyards in the blue-tinged shadows of Mont Sainte-Odile, when Roussillon rises up on its red peaks, when the outline of the abbey of Conques emerges out its canyons, the notion of time is abolished, the borders of reality fade and we enter the magic kingdom of our childhood dreams. The villages of those "lands" dear to Fernand Braudel weave a multicolored thread in a tapestry of styles that reflect the incredible diversity of "the beautiful France." These villages continue to hint at the fortunes and misfortunes of a disappearing rural way of life, without whose memory we would be but chaff in the pernicious winds of modernity. But they also hint at the good taste of our departed country bourgeoisie.

It's the History of France that unfolds as the voyager, neglecting the commonplace international tourist stops, commemorates the feudal age at the black basalt walls of Salers, ardent faith before the church at Talmont and facing the estuary, the saga of the Resistance on the Ile de Sein. From the hilltops of Vézelay a spirit breathes: it comes to rest in the Auge valley with its dappled herds and in the orchards and pastures of Beuvron. In short, this is an exotic way to invoke the humble genius of a people who have always had in their hearts a sense of beauty and privacy. Have they lost the secret of this harmony and grace which emanates from every corner? It is to be feared.

Faced with a contemporary aesthetics that saddens us, to put it mildly, I can't think of a better education for our urban and suburban-dwelling children than to show them the houses huddled around a steepled church, a dungeon or a monastery, hand-built by men who spontaneously celebrated a life that we search for in vain: the marriage of the everyday and the sublime. We are tired and bored with everything, because we have seen it all, but the final enchantment is within the reach of all who desire it.

Denis TILLINAC

CONTENTS

THE NORTH, PICARDY, CHAMPAGNE AND THE ARDENNES

The North region reflects the great and eventful past of the duchy of Burgundy, the empire of Charles V, the Holy Roman emperor. The plains of Flanders by the North Sea, the hills of Artois and the enclosed fields of the Hainault and the Asvenois all bear witness to this rich history. "Champagne and Flanders are the only regions to rival Italy in the Middle Ages in terms of history. Flanders has the poet Froissart and the statesman Commynes as counterparts to both Villoni and Machiavelli," once wrote Michelet, the French Romantic historian. The minstrel Adam de la Halle, famous for his contribution to the Ars Nova, was born in Arras; Valenciennes was the birthplace of the painter Antoine Watteau and the sculptor Jean-Baptiste Carpeaux. Henri Matisse originated from Cateau-Cambrésis. *Under the Sun of Satan* and other novels by the great Catholic writer Georges Bernanos are set in Artois, and the famed novelist Marguerite Yourcenar retraces her childhood memories in the North in *How Many Years*, the second volume of her complete autobiography.

The heart of such cities as Lille, Arras, Béthune or Douai still beats in olden squares paced by the clocks of the ancient belfries. Gabled houses with elaborate façades, fine examples of Flemish Gothic style, surround the squares dating from the golden age of the northern clothiers. These houses still host the centuries-old charity fairs, "kermesses," once rythming the life of the country. They give rise to spectacular parades of giant mannequins, each the symbol of a city. Many other such traditions have survived in the form of the famed Calais lace or the Cambrai sweets known as "bêtises." Neighboring villages boast low, old red ochre or whitewashed brick houses. The presence of the now abandoned mines still marks the northern landscape. New vegetation grows on the old black tips towering over long rows of mining cottages in the vicinity of Lens.

Parfondeval

The two red brick towers and the arch marking the entrance to the church remind us of the long belligerent past of the region. The village is set in the fertile and often coveted country of Thiérache that lies north of the Aisne, in between the Oise and the Sambre rivers.

Bergues, a few miles from Dunkerque, is nestled against medieval ramparts fortified under Louis XIV and surrounded by water-filled moats. The belfry, the canal bordering the village and the 18th century mill erected a bit further off, in Pitgam, are all built in the Flemish style. The same character is

echoed in Cassel, a little more to the South. Beautiful mansions, one of which housed Marshall Foch and his staff in 1915, remain along the cobbled square of this village built on a hill. In addition, several mills have survived the onslaught of time in the windswept country of Steenvorde.

The high cliffs of Blanc-Nez and Gris-Nez jut out over the sea along the Opale coast and the fine sand dunes stretch out to the Sommes River. Elegant villas set in between sea and forest enhance the Wimereux, Hardelot, and Le Touquet sea resorts, where long beaches attract both bathing and sand-yachting enthusiasts.

Close to the harbor of Etaples, Montreuil rises over the beautiful valley of the Canche River. Erected in the Middle Ages, the citadel and the ramparts enclosing the town were rebuilt many times, due to the destructive onslaughts of the troops of Charles the Fifth of Spain. A stroll in town takes one through cobbled alleyways to the street Clape-en-Bas bordered by houses with vivid colored shutters and to the Saint-Saulve abbey. Montreuil is where the great 19th century French writer Victor Hugo set his famous novel *Les Misérables*. During the Hundred Years' War, the surrounding country of Artois was the scene for the decisive battle of Azincourt, won by the English king Henry the Fourth in 1415. Inner feuds between the provinces of Burgundy and Armagnac had contributed to the fall of the French army. A museum stages the grounds where the different episodes of this legendary battle took place. The French Romantic historian Michelet draws attention to the historical and artistic legacy of the region: "Picardy seemingly embodies the history of ancient France. Royalty resided successively in Soissons, Crépy, Verberie, and Attigny during the reign of Queen Frédégonde and King Charles le Chauve. Later, the nascent republic was assisted in its painful and hurried delivery by many a native from Picardy such as Condorcet, Desmoulins, or Baboeuf, all great figures of the French Revolution." He further points out that the classic 17th century painters Claude Lorrain and Poussin, the 18th century composer Lesueur, the French Renaissance sculptor Goujon, the 17th century architect Mansart, and the 18th century painter David all originated from the northern provinces.

Le Crotoy and Saint-Valéry-sur-Somme frame a magnificent bay. Sheep graze on the surrounding meadows and birds nest in the vast reserve of the Marquenterre estate, restored from the surrounding swamps. Fish teem in the lazy waters of the Somme flowing across a valley of marshlands from Abbeville to Péronne. Small plots of land criss-crossed by canals range across former marshes on the outskirts of Amiens. Fruits, flowers and vegetables have been grown there since the Middle Ages. Several decisive events took place in this region during the last two world wars. Numerous churches and abbeys are scattered across the country, such as the vast cathedral of Amiens, a superb example of the Gothic style, or the collegiate church of Abbeville, adorned with a flamboyant and finely sculpted façade. The villages of Saint-Riquier, Corbie or Bray-sur-Somme are also endowed with beautiful religious monuments. In the valley of Authie lies Lucheux, a village crowned by the vestiges of a castle, of which the two pepper-box towers still remain. Saint-Quentin, the largest town of the Aisne, is the birthplace of Quentin de La Tour, the famous French pastelist. He has left a series of remarkably lifelike portraits of the great figures of his time, such as Madame de Pompadour, former mistress to King Louis XV and the great 18th century philosophers. "Unknown to them, I work my way deep inside them and bring out their entire being."

Gerberoy

A profusion of flowers graces this charming and beautifully restored village in the spring. This picture, taken during the winter and at dusk, highlights the authentic medieval character of this fortified village, formerly the scene of many a battle in the era of William the Conqueror.

Thiérache, land of pastures and enclosed fields, stretches out to the east between the Oise and the Sambre rivers. The much reputed local cheese is still made there following a recipe invented nine hundred years ago by the monks of the abbey of Maroilles. Fortified churches spread across the country, originally built in an effort to protect the inhabitants from invaders. Such villages as Plomion, Jeantes,

Renneval and Dohis, situated between Guise and Parfondeval, have preserved these solid monuments built mostly in brick and flanked by turrets, machicolations and dungeons. Dohis also boasts beautiful old houses with timber-framed façades. The warm red-brick tones of the fortified church of Parfondeval are echoed in the red and brown hues that predominate throughout the surrounding village.

South of Soissons, on the outskirts of the Retz Forest, lie the remnants of the 12th century Cistercian abbey of Longpont, later reshaped in the 18th century. Turrets top the fortified door heralding the entrance to the village. This vestige of fortification bears witness to the times when the once prosperous abbey was coveted by the Normans, the Burgundians and the English. Close by, in the heart of the forest is Villers-Cotterêts where, in 1569, the French King Françis I formally established French as the official language to be used in all administrative and judicial documents, up to then written in Latin. He also introduced the Civil Status, entrusted to the religious authorities until the French Revolution. Villers-Cotterêts is

where Alexandre Dumas, the French 19th century novelist and author of *The Count of Monte Cristo*, spent the first twenty years of his life before embarking on a literary career in Paris. A few miles away, in Ferté-Milon, the great classic French 17th century playwright Racine was born in 1639. The 17th century poet Jean de La Fontaine, famous for his fables, once used to visit his fiancée in this village dominating the Ourcq River.

Close to Normandy, the village of Gerberoy was once the scene of many battles among the English, the Normans and the French. The ramparts enclosing this picturesque village, set in the Oise valley, are covered in flowers in the spring and are now potent reminders of those harrowing times.

Cobbled streets, old covered markets, half-timbered houses and splendid terrace gardens laid out on the former site of the fortress enhance this village, one of the most beautiful of its kind to be put on the historical register. On the edge of the Compiègne forest, situated by a romantic lake, Pierrefonds prides itself on a fortified castle. This medieval stronghold was entirely rebuilt by the 19th century restorer Viollet-le-Duc for the benefit of Napoleon III, who used it as his imperial residence. "There is not a town or a village in Champagne that is not blessed with a character of its own," once wrote Victor Hugo. Champagne enjoyed great prosperity during the Middle Ages, thanks to its being at a crossroads between the great trading centers of Flanders and Italy.

Reims and Epernay are today the most renowned wine capitals of the world, famous for their prestigious cellars. Champagne wine had been the object of much relish for centuries before the secret for achieving the sparkling bubbles, otherwise known as double fermentation, was discovered at the end of the 17th century. Dom Pérignon, prior of the abbey of Hautvillers, in the Montagne de Reims, has always been considered to be the inventor of this method. Although today many doubt this belief, his name will always be associated with the history of the making of champagne. Beautiful half-timbered houses, hallmarks of the once flourishing Renaissance, still grace the old districts of such cities as Troyes, where they have been particularly well-maintained, or the villages of Saint-Amand-sur-Fion, Puellemontier or Chaource, the latter famous for its cheese. East of Troyes, in Champagne Humide, timber-frames adorn the 16th century churches of Lentilles, as well as those, as beautiful but simpler, in Bailly-le-Franc. Villages scatter across the region amidst enclosed fields, woods and meadows.

Further north, the hills of the Argonne recall the dark days of the French Revolution: Varennes, where the royal family was arrested after having been recognized at the stage-inn of Sainte-Menehould. The Argonne forest also carries strong memories from the first World War.

At the beginning of the 12th century, Bernard de Fontaine, who was to become Saint Bernard, founded a Cistercian abbey whose exceptional spiritual influence was centered at Clairvaux, near Bar-sur-Aube, home of the philosopher Gaston Bachelard. A few miles away, the village of Colombey-les-Deux-Eglises is closely linked to the memory of General de Gaulle, who retired there to spend the latter part of his life on his estate, La Boisserie. In Langres, on the borders of Burgundy, the 18th century writer Diderot was born into a family of wealthy cutlers.

To the north of Reims, the Ardennes region has always been a land of migrations, a thoroughfare exposed to invasions. The castle of Bouillon, the fortifications of Rocroi and the stronghold at Sedan bear witness to this turbulent past. The shades of the poets Paul Verlaine and Arthur Rimbaud haunt these roads. Verlaine lived in Juniville and Coulommes, two villages near Rethel, where he taught English, and near Roche, where Rimbaud wrote *A Season in Hell*. Charleville-Mézières where Rimbaud was born and is buried, has become a place of pilgrimage for all the admirers of the poet "who walked on the wind."

Ville-Dommange and Sacy

The view of these two villages in Champagne shows the traditional features of the French farming landscape. The green hills and the houses carefully grouped together in the shadow of the church tower seem to proclaim that rural life will always stay the same.

ALSACE LORRAINE

"The Rhine, the Rhine is drunk where it mirrors the vineyards" wrote the poet Apollinaire in his Rhineland poems, harking back to the legend of the beautiful Lorelei "the blond witch with eyes of precious stones". The river, which today forms the natural border between France and Germany, has always nourished the imagination of the literati on both banks. Hölderlin and Alexandre Dumas, Erckmann and Chatrian have all extolled the beauty and mystery of this land, long coveted by the countries on both sides of the river. Many of the Alsatian villages have retained the charm of past centuries as they nestle among luxuriant vineyards, woods and orchards.

Strasbourg is a lively city where the Council of Europe has its headquarters. The area called "Little France," built along a canal, has remained undisturbed since it was inhabited by tanners and fishermen centuries ago. Its counterpart in Colmar is called "Little Venice," although its half-timbered houses are typically Alsatian.

From Wissenbourg in the north to Mulhouse in the south, the Alsatian landscape is extremely varied: the plain of the Rhine to the east, the foothills of the Vosges Mountains to the west are followed by the "balloon-shaped" hills around Guebwiller and the plateaux of the Sundgau.

The villages scattered along the wine road in Alsace are among the most picturesque in the region. From Marlenheim to Thann, across the Bas-Rhin and the Haut-Rhin, their church spires signal the vineyards where famous white wines are produced. The meticulously kept, half-timbered houses with their shining white or softly colored fronts, and the streets and balconies decked with flowers, combine to give these villages the freshness of unfolding blossoms.

Here and there fortifications appear to remind the traveler that, in the course of its history, this country was claimed by French and Germanic rulers as well as by the Duchy of Burgundy. Near the lovely town of Obernai,

Hunawihr

In the fall, the wine road erupts into fireworks of colors dominated by the red and gold of the vineyards. Alsace has no less than seven wines (both red and white) of controlled origin. An outstanding feature of this village is the imposing fortified church where the population took shelter in times of unrest. The remarkable six-sided wall around it is two hundred years older than the church: it dates from the 14th century. The fact that, architecturally, both the church and the city hall, built in the same period, were accorded the same importance is a token of the good relations that existed between the clergy and the State in Alsace.

inside the ramparts of Boersch, a paved square is graced by an ornate Renaissance well. In Mittelbergheim, ancient houses crowd around two churches, one Catholic, the other Protestant. Yet another walled city, Dambach-la-Ville, lies at the foot of a hill. Its central square, surrounded by timber-framed houses and the step-gabled town hall, make it a beautiful example of the Alsatian Renaissance.

A little to the south, at Bergheim, the round towers, erected in the 14th century by the Habsburg family, still protect the beautiful houses of the wine growers. Beyond Ribeauvillé, where the traditional wine festival is still held in September, the small village of

Hunawihr is home to a stork farm. Then, in the heart of the wine-growing country, where Riesling is made, an elegant church spire marks the city of Riquewihr. It was fortified in the 13th century by a double wall which is still standing. One of the gates in the inner wall is guarded by a high tower, built of a mixture of stone and half-timbering, which harbors a museum of local history. This tower, the Dolder, has become the symbol of the city. To reach it, one follows the Grand-Rue, lined with beautiful medieval and Renaissance houses and crossed by narrow alleys and passages. Fountains, old signs identifying craftsmen or wine growers, wooden balconies with carved balustrades and sculpted beams decorate the adjoining streets.

In the valley of the Weiss, Kaysersberg, i.e. the "Emperor's mountain," has since Roman times been a strategic crossing point between the Rhine and Gaul. The ruins of a medieval castle dominate the city, which has kept its original character. The ancient half-timbered and corbeled houses with their high, steep roofs are perfectly maintained. This is where Albert Schweitzer was born in 1875. He began as a clergyman in Strasbourg, studied medicine there and later, during the First World War, he founded a hospital in Lambarene, Gabon, where after some time, he settled for good. He was awarded the Nobel Peace Prize in 1952. His writing includes works on philosophy and musicology.

On the outskirts of Colmar, the lovely houses of Niedermorschwihr and Turckheim are often decorated on the street side with bay windows and glass balconies, also found in many other villages. These bay windows appear again in Eguisheim, a marvelous village, encircling an old fortress and surrounded by the ruins of the "five castles road."

Beside these wine-growing centers of excellence, other villages are just as charming; for example, Hunspach, Zutzendorf, Lorentzen and Buswiller are composed of large farms whose buildings surround a central courtyard. Sewen lies close to the Alsace regional park and the Doller Valley with its lakes. Hirtzbach, in the

Valley of the Ill, Grentzingen with its ocher-colored houses or, to the south, Ferrette, former capital of the Sundgau, all have the same half-timbered houses lining pleasant squares and streets. The castles in Alsace contain untold treasures, and since they are often built on the heights, as are Haut-Barr and Haut-Koenigsbourg, they command magnificent views of the surrounding country.

Extending from the western slope of the Vosges Mountains to the Champagne region, the Lorraine consists of a succession of peaks and plains, crossed by rivers that give their names to its three districts: Meurthe, Moselle and Meuse. Lorraine, like Alsace, has seen many battles in the course of its history. They are commemorated in

foundations from the 4th century. In the 13th century, the dukes of Lorraine chose Nancy as their capital because it was situated in the heart of their lands. The city continued to develop until, in the 18th century, King Stanislas Leszczynski undertook far-reaching and lavish transformations. Among others, the square was enclosed by the famous wrought-iron railings designed by Jean Lamour. Due to the glass-maker Emile Gallé, the "école de Nancy" became a driving force in the Art Nouveau movement at the beginning of the 20th century, just as Lunéville had been for glazed earthenware. In Epinal, close to the basilica, there remains a group of chapter houses and an ancient square lined with arcades. Epinal is known for its manufacture of well-loved colored-prints created by Jean-Charles Pellerin, two hundred years ago; these prints were very popular during the entire 19th century and are still prized for their naïve design and coloring.

The Lorraine villages have a less distinctive architecture than those in Alsace but they are filled with vestiges of the past. Hattonchâtel, built on the hills above the Meuse, was founded by a bishop of Verdun in the 9th century. Adjoining the church, a tower belonging to the ancient fortress escaped the destruction ordered by cardinal Richelieu. The church, flanked by a cloister, shelters a statue of the Virgin and remarkable altarpieces. In August, Hattonchâtel celebrates the festival of the mirabelle plum which, together with the blueberry, is the chief fruit of the region. A bit further south, Saint-Mihiel is the birthplace of the 16th century sculptor, Ligier Richier, whose work can be seen all over Lorraine. The church of Saint-Etienne in Mihiel has his wonderful *Burial of Christ*.

Vaucouleurs is the town where Joan of Arc persuaded the king's governor to give her a few companions in arms to launch her crusade against the English. Her native village, Domrémy, preserves the memory of her exploits, particularly in the basilica of Bois-Chenu, which was built on the spot where Joan is said to have heard the divine call to arms.

Somewhat to the east there is a hill, between Sion and Vaudémont, which the author Maurice Barrès called the "Hill of Inspiration." This hill dominating the Lorraine plateau has been a place of worship ever since the Celtic era, and during the Franco-German wars it was a symbol of hope and unity for many of the inhabitants of Lorraine.

Verdun and in many other places. During the First World War, Bar-le-Duc was the starting point of the "Sacred Road" that brought supplies to Verdun. In the upper part of the city, around the Saint-Pierre square, beautiful old houses remain, dominated by the Saint-Etienne church. Metz is the birthplace of the poet Paul Verlaine. Its position at a crossroad – the confluence of the rivers Seille and Moselle – made it an important trading center in Gallo-Roman times and, in 561, the capital of the "Eastern Kingdom" (Austrasia). The city has had a great number of churches, the most interesting being: the cathedral Saint-Etienne with its magnificent stained-glass windows and Saint-Pierre-aux-Nonnains, several times rebuilt but with

Marville

This peaceful Lorraine village is situated in a predominantly farming area. It was formerly the most important city in the northern part of the Meuse region and was called the Major Villa by the Romans. It sits on top of a hill that commands the valleys of the Othair and the Gédon. From the 13th century to the second half of the 17th century, Marville had the privilege of being a free city that attracted rich merchants. And the fact that Spanish regiments were stationed there from 1560 did not change its status. The Spanish contributed to the village by building beautiful Renaissance houses which can still be seen today. Louis XIV reconquered the region and ordered the dismantling of the city walls. The church of Saint-Nicolas is a remarkable example of 14th century Gothic art, although it was started in the preceding century and further embellished during the Renaissance. High above Marville, the cemetery of the Saint-Hilaire chapel contains treasures of funerary art.

Near Nancy, the basilica of Saint-Nicolas-de-Port has always had a special aura: it harbors a relic of the saint, who is particularly close to the hearts of the people of Lorraine and of all children. Saint Nicolas, who is credited with the resurrection of three children, is here in the north, merged with the figure of Father Christmas. On the 6th of December, some cities in the Lorraine region organize processions in whose midst the effigy of Saint Nicolas is carried through the streets. Saint Nicolas also houses curiosities of a more prosaic kind, such as a brewery museum.

In the Mosel region, near the border with Luxemburg, some medieval villages still retain parts of their fortifications. Rodemack, the "Carcassonne of Lorraine," is still completely surrounded by ramparts from the 15th century enclosing its narrow streets. Besides the fortress, there is a lovely chapel as well as simple votive crosses gracing a square or a crossroads. Sierck-les-Bains, on the Mosel River, is a meeting place for all river-boating enthusiasts. The remnants of its medieval fortifications, its ruined castle and houses with 18th century façades, have, by chance, escaped the destruction wrought on it by the Second World War.

Bitche, near the German border and the castle of Falkenstein, nestles at the foot of its red sandstone citadel. This part of the Northern Vosges natural reserve has been the center of crystal manufacturing since the 16th century. The master glass-blowers in Saint-Louis-lès-Bitche still create pieces renowned for their elegance, as do those in Baccarat, between Lunéville and Saint-Dié.

Another tradition, that of paper-making, lives on in the Vosges region. The paper mill in Arches, near Epinal, has a history that goes back five hundred years. It belonged to the 18th century playwright Beaumarchais, who used the Arche paper to print, in Germany, the complete works of Voltaire, who, at the time, was forbidden to publish in France. The southern part of the Vosges region, around Gérardmer, has a magnificent landscape of forests, lakes, streams and waterfalls. Water is everywhere and, further south, it is used for curative and relaxing purposes in numerous spas: Vittel, Contrexéville, Plombières. The Romans were the first to visit Bourbonne-les-Bains and Plombières. From the Middle Ages onward, the baths at Plombières enjoyed a high reputation, but their heyday came with Emperor Napoleon III, who enjoyed spending time there.

Riquewihr

Riquewihr nestling in the heart of the Alsace wine country is the land of the Riesling, one of the most prestigious white wines. Half-timbered houses and carved wooden balconies full of flowers, fountains and old-fashioned shop signs line its main street. The Dolder tower, one of the outstanding features of the city, formed part of the 13th century ramparts. Today it houses a museum of local history.

NORMANDY ILE-DE-FRANCE

"Paris, Rouen, Le Havre make one single city whose main street is the Seine... The Seine marches on and carries the thoughts of France, of Paris, to Normandy, to the ocean, to England and far-away America" wrote Jules Michelet. The links between Normandy and Ile-de-France have a long history, dating from the 3rd century B.C., when the Seine was the only thoroughfare *en route* to the tin that had to be fetched from the other side of the English Channel. From the 9th century on, the Seine was the route by which the Vikings sailed all the way to Paris. On a happier side, the precursors of impressionist painting, Camille Corot and Eugène Boudin, born in Honfleur, tried to capture the light of the Normandy coast and of the green banks of the river. The list of painters who followed in their footsteps is as plentiful as the subjects to which they applied their brushes: Pissarro, Sisley, Monet, Seurat, Signac, Van Dongen... Landscapes, the play of light on the water and the sky, beaches, sailboats and skiffs: the mood of their paintings recalls the world of Maupassant, who, among others, often wrote about Normandy and its people in his short stories.

Where the country is flat, the towns and villages of Normandy spread out across the vast meadows; in the hilly regions, they are scattered over a checkerboard of enclosed fields. Although the traditional Normandy houses are half-timbered, made of cob and wood, they are not all like that. Since the environment offers a variety of materials, on the coast and inland (limestone, pebbles, shale, granite, clay), the inhabitants have used them all to build monuments and homes, achieving a variety equal to that of the landscape. Wood, available in abundance, has also served to construct the walls of the thatched-roof houses. Of late, the thatch has been replaced by slate and the wood by bricks, but the fronts of the houses often remain half-timbered.

Barfleur

When entering Normandy through Barfleur, at the eastern point of the Cotentin Peninsula, one follows the route of the invading Normans. One also follows in the wake of William the Conqueror, since it was from this port, formerly the most important one on the coast, that he set sail to conquer England. Today, Barfleur is a small fishing and pleasure-craft port whose granite houses, typical of the Cotentin Peninsula, are tangible evidence of the solid Norman traditions.

Normandy suffered heavily during the Second World War, but it has preserved or restored a large part of its most precious architectural heritage. Abbeys and fortresses, churches and manor houses, small picturesque ports and villages are scattered over a landscape where the sea and the fields, farmland and vast meadows combine to make a harmonious whole.

In the north, Upper Normandy, with Rouen as its focal point, is divided by the Seine into the Caux and the Auge regions. In the south, Lower Normandy, where Caen

is the main center–covers "Norman Switzerland" and the Cotentin Peninsula. On the border with Picardy, the lush vegetation of the Bray region, renowned for its cheeses and its cider, differs sharply from the chalk of its neighbor, the Caux, on the Channel coast. It stretches from Tréport to Le Havre and its white cliffs have given rise to its name: the Alabaster Coast. All along this coast, ports and bathing beaches follow each other: Dieppe, Varengeville, Veules-les-Roses, all the way to Etretat, renowned for its spectacular views as well as for the exploits of Arsène Lupin inside the famous "needle," in the story by Maurice Leblanc. Further north, there is Fécamp, where the writer Maupassant once lived. South, at the mouth of the Seine, lies Le Havre, the fifth busiest European port, birthplace of such writers as Bernardin de Saint-Pierre and Raymond Queneau.

Upstream of Le Havre, at the point where the river starts to meander, stands Villequier, which has a museum devoted to the writer Victor Hugo. This is the place where his daughter Léopoldine and her husband drowned a few months after their wedding.

Two of the most famous French abbeys rise above the natural park of the Brotonne forest: Saint-Wandrille, a Benedictine abbey with the remains of a magnificent cloister, and Jumiège, whose imposing nave has withstood the test of time. Both were founded in the 7th century and became extremely influential in the Middle Ages. Further up, on another bend in the Seine, there is Rouen, the birthplace of Corneille, Fontenelle and Flaubert and described by a fellow writer, Maupassant, in a collection of short stories: "Rouen, the city of churches, of gothic spires as ornate as ivory carvings; facing us, Saint-Sever, the borough of the manufacturers, raises its thousand smoking chimneys in the face of the thousand sacred pinnacles of the old city." This mixture of intense activity and remarkable architecture can still be felt in the city today. It has preserved, around one of the most beautiful Gothic cathedrals, part of the ancient city, which has been superbly restored. To the east of Rouen, sheltered by the great forest of Lyons, lies a lovely Normandy village, Lyons-la-Forêt, where, at one time, the English kings resided. The composer Maurice Ravel liked to stay there, and this is where he composed some of his music. One can still visit the house of Benserade, the poet who, with the composer Lully, wrote librettos for the court of Louis XIV.

In another bend of the Seine, Les Andelys is dominated by the ruins of the fortress of Château-Gaillard, built by Richard the Lion-Hearted in the 12th century. Further upstream, near Vernon, the little village of Giverny is known across the world as the place where the painter Monet had his house and his garden, which in the spring, sparkles with all the colors of his palette. Around 1880 the painter came to settle in this pink and green house nestling among the flowers on the border of Normandy and Ile-de-France, and he died there surrounded by his loved ones in 1926. South of the Seine, the Auge region surrounds its capital, Lisieux. This is the Normandy of pastures and orchards, a landscape of small fields and hedgerows, harboring the secrets of how to make cider, calvados and cheeses such as Livarot, Pont-l'Evêque and Camembert. Around the cities and villages, beautiful manor-houses and large farms grace the countryside. Among the delightful and picturesque villages, Crèvecoeur-en-Auge, Saint-Germain-de-Livet and many others, Beuvron-en-Auge is probably the best-known. Its houses, the most ancient ones dating from the 17th century, have bright-colored roof-tiles and are clustered around the market square. Their fronts are half-timbered, decorated with a variety of designs whose charm is appreciated by an enthusiastic throng of weekend visitors looking for bargains among the local crafts and antiques. The Auge region also boasts a famous abbey, Bec-Hellouin, built near the coast in the 11th century.

This "Flowered Coast" has a number of very popular seaside resorts, appreciated particularly by the Parisians since the Second Empire. Honfleur figures in many paintings by Eugène Boudin and by the members of the Barbizon School as well as in works by English painters who crossed the Channel to find inspiration. Further south lie Trouville with its beaches of fine sand, the highly sophisticated Deauville and Houlgate with its villas hidden behind screens of greenery and, finally, Cabourg to which the French novelist Proust, a frequent guest of its Grand-Hôtel, gave the name Balbec in his celebrated literary masterpiece *Remembrance of Things Past*.

The entrance to Lower-Normandy is through the country of Ouche, now a land of woods and cattle-farming but formerly populated by blacksmiths. The Norman part of the Perche region has, for decades, been devoted to horses and many of the estates have become stud farms.

South of Caen, "Norman Switzerland" becomes more hilly and the river Orne winds through a country of enclosed fields. The abbey of the Men and the abbey of the Ladies, the two most beautiful buildings in Caen, recall the love between William the Conqueror and his wife Mathilde, their founders. In order to admire the famous tapestry that bears the name of Queen Mathilde, one has to travel to Bayeux, inland from the beaches where the allied landings during the Second World War have left their indelible mark on the coast and country around Arromanches and Sainte-Mère-l'Eglise.

Beuvron-en-Auge

First the half-timbered houses appeared in Alsace, then in Normandy. The architectural similarities, on the same latitude in eastern and western France, reveal the prosperity of a class of professionals and merchants during the Renaissance.

On the Cotentin Peninsula, the houses are already tinged with a color that heralds Brittany as, for example, in Barfleur, a small seaside resort with granite houses which was a favorite with the painter Signac. Saint-Sauveur-le-Vicomte, in the heart of the peninsula, was the birthplace of Barbey d'Aurevilly, a colorful dandy and witty pamphleteer.

The Cotentin is a major producer of milk, perry (fermented pear juice) and cider. In the south, around the bay of Mont Saint-Michel, sheep are raised on the salt marshes, producing the salt-marsh lamb that delights gourmets. The magnificent abbey is now situated in Brittany (much to the distate of the Normans) because of a whim of the river marking the frontier between the two provinces.

The Ile-de-France region cannot boast such beautifully preserved villages as Normandy. The population explosion, the growth of the city of Paris and new industrial sites have left little space for them. In the area surrounding the capital, vestiges of the history of France are more numerous than the remnants of its rural past. Castles and splendid parks abound (Versailles, Saint-Germain-en-Laye, Saint-Cloud, Vaux-le-Vicomte, Champs-sur-Marne, to name but a few). One has to move farther and farther away from the city to find any picturesque village streets. They exist, however, in the Vexin region, in the Chevreuse Valley, in the Val d'Oise, Beauce and Brie regions, and they are permeated by the memories of painters who put them on their canvases as well as of the farmers and craftsmen who brought them to life.

In the Vexin region, between the valleys of the Epte, the Viosne and the Seine, villages of solid stone houses are surrounded by vast grain fields. Moussy, Giry and Wy are clustered around their beautiful churches with manor-houses and small castles scattered in the vicinity: Vétheuil, La Roche-Guyon, Vigny and Villarceau are where the memory of the fascinating Ninon de Lenclos still lingers.

In Auvers-sur-Oise, it is the figure of Van Gogh that dominates the streets, the church and the fields that he loved to paint. In 1890, Van Gogh came to live here in the village inn, across the street from the town hall, and set to work, incessantly painting the country and its inhabitants until he committed suicide a few months later. Two other villages not far from Auvers, Valmondois and Hérouville, also inspired painters such as Cézanne and Pissarro, who had recommended Van Gogh to Doctor Gachet and who lived for a while in Pontoise.

The Chevreuse Valley also harbors many delightful sites. Hidden among woods and in small valleys, the banks of the rivers Yvette, Bièvre and Essonne reveal scores of elegant mansions.

In this region, where grain and watercress are grown, villages are still centered around their old covered markets. Around 1850, a few painters settled in Barbizon, a tranquil farming community which suddenly became famous. Théodore Rousseau, Millet and Diaz came to live in Barbizon, and Corot, Daumier and Daubigny paid frequent visits. The artists in Barbizon,

near Fontainebleau, did not create a specific style, but their habit of painting nature "from nature" made them known as the "Barbizon School."

The narrow streets around the inn of Père Ganne, where the visiting painters used to stay, are today transformed into a museum village. The whole area has inspired artists: a few miles away, the chapel in Milly-la-Forêt was decorated by Jean Cocteau, and Sisley chose Moret-sur-Loing, beautifully mirrored in the river, as the place to live until the end of his life. To the northeast, the Grand-Morin Valley separates French

Brie from Brie in Champagne. Here, the vast wheat fields and meadows are interspersed with large farm-houses around square courtyards. Famous cheeses are made at Melun, Meaux and Coulommiers.

Villages like Vaudoy-en-Brie and Voulton have preserved their rural habitat and memories of the past (fountains and remnants of dovecotes). The castle of Ferrières was, in 1870, the scene of an attempted truce in the Franco-Prussian war. The castle of Guermantes was built in the 17th century and inspired the French writer Marcel Proust.

BRITTANY
THE LOIRE COUNTRY

The historical places in Brittany combine age-old megalithic vestiges of ancient Celtic culture with abundant evidence that this has, for centuries, been a much coveted land. The castles and churches as well as the modest village houses are mostly built of local granite and shale, and roofed with slate from the Black Mountain. Among the great ports and vast forests, university cities and market gardens, Brittany hides innumerable small communities where legends linger and history speaks.

The charm of Paimpont, on the border between the Ille-et-Villaine and Morbihan regions, is enhanced by the mythical forest of Brocéliande that enfolds it. The name of every street and square recalls the adventures of King Arthur, the sorcerer Merlin, the Lady of the Lake, Viviane, and the eternal struggle between good and evil. The castle of Trécesson, the chaos of the Val sans Retour, the springs and the megaliths have, since the Middle Ages, echoed with stories of battles between dragons and valiant knights.

This medieval atmosphere reigns in the old cities of Rennes, Fougères, Dinan and Dol, centering around their cathedrals. In Vitré, the old city has also retained beautiful wood-fronted houses along the medieval streets confined inside the city walls, at the foot of the castle, topped by pepper-pot towers. The castle of les Rochers, close by, belonged to Madame de Sévigné, whose abundant correspondence paints a detailed picture of local events and her own life in Brittany. The writer Chateaubriand, born in Saint-Malo, describes in his *Memoirs* his childhood years at Combourg, his family seat, a castle now open to the public, and completely unchanged from the past.

In the Côte-d'Armor region, Moncontour is a beautiful example of a well preserved medieval town with its alleys sheltered by the remnants of the 11th century city walls, once dismantled on the order of Cardinal de Richelieu.

Locronan

The sturdy granite houses lining the village square recall the times when hemp was woven into sails for the East India Company and the English, Spanish and Dutch navies. The church of Saint-Ronan, from the 15th century, dominates the village with its square tower next to the 16th century chapel of the Penity. This chapel shelters the recumbent sculpture of the patron saint of the city, Saint Ronan, who is said to have introduced flax farming to the area. Locronan is an important religious center, as are Sainte-Anne-la-Palud and farther away, Sainte-Anne-d'Auray. The worship of Saint Anne is widespread in Brittany and sometimes confused with the memory of Queen Anne of Brittany.

On the jagged Emerald Coast, ports, beaches and cliffs offer a great variety of scenery, whose common feature is the blue-green sea, streaked with ribbons of tiny islands. Saint-Malo, brimful of memories from its pirate past, is followed westward by Dinard, a sophisticated, very British resort. Then, Saint-Briac, Saint-Jacut, Le Guildo, Cape Fréhel, Erquy and others, all the way to the Trégor coast, which was formerly the departure point for the boats fishing off the coast of Iceland. Near Paimpol, at the point of Arcouest, one can take a boat to the island of Bréhat. This little island divided between the rocks and moors in the north and a tiny village in the south, is a small world all of its own, without cars or big buildings. Along its narrow streets, parasol pines and fig trees shelter houses surrounded by hydrangeas and mimosa. Bréhat is built of the pink granite that has given its name to a lovely part of the coastline. Still further west, between Perros-Guirrec and Trébeurden, the rocks are sculpted by the wind and the sea into extraordinary shapes. Inland, many villages still have their ancient chapels graced by splendid objects of religious art. The chapel at Kerfons harbors a marvelously carved rood screen from the 15th century. Near Guingamp, the church at Loc Envel has a vaulted ceiling shaped like the upturned hull of a ship, and a beautifully ornate interior. As is often the case in Brittany, the beauty of the building comes from craftsmanship. The material is often wood, superbly crafted by marine woodworkers.

shrubs grow on the islands between the fields, crisscrossed by stone walls behind which the sheep graze. The houses on the islands are low and built of stone, their backs to the wind, and their shutters are often painted blue. This tradition is perpetuated on the island of Sein. Not far from the Bay of Brest, Le Faou gets its name from the Breton word for "beech." The wood used to transit through this formerly very busy port which is now almost totally silted up. Its 16th century houses, with their bay windows, are clustered around a lovely church with a lacework spire.

One of the most picturesque Breton villages is, without a doubt, Locronan, which was the domain of the weavers from the Renaissance to the 19th century. The Finistère region has written its maritime history in stone: in Penmarch, fish and ships decorate the church façades. On Penmarch Point stands one of the most powerful lighthouses in France. In the surrounding country, the women lace-makers from the Pont-l'Abbé region carry on the tradition of wearing the high lace headdresses, but now only on special feast days.

Situated on a river with a few remaining mills and dominated by the Bois-d'Amour, Pont-Aven continues its artistic tradition through its many art galleries. Gauguin came here in 1886 to join a community of artists, charmed by the beauty of the area. His presence further increased the reputation and the numbers of the "Pont-Aven School." The museum that now houses their work is located close to the inn where they used to stay.

Across from Lorient, with its many memories of the great adventures of the East India Company, the island of Groix offers its green valleys, high cliffs and sandy cover. Its church is crowned by a weathervane that recalls generations of island history: the traditional rooster is replaced by a tuna. The aptly named Belle-Ile (Beautiful Isle) is much larger and farther from the coast, off the Quiberon Peninsula. Its coastal villages –Le Palais, Sauzon and, on the "Côte sauvage", Port-Donnant and Port-Goulphar– give shelter to pleasure craft. The caves hollowed out of the cliffs "fiery red and brown with white stripes" enchanted the writer Flaubert, while the "needles" of Port-Coton (rocks sticking out of the sea) inspired Monet. On Belle-Isle's two little sister islands, Houat and Hoëdic, small white houses crouch along the twisting alleys.

La Grande Brière, the outpost of the region around Nantes, was formerly an inlet sprinkled with islands. Filled-in by the alluvium of the Loire River, it became a marshland that was painstakingly drained by human labor, enabling the

The parish enclosures are among the greatest treasures of the religious and architectural heritage in Brittany. There are some seventy of them, mainly in the Finistère region: Saint-Thégonnec, Guimiliau, Plougastel among others. They were all created between the 15th and the 17th centuries. The enclosures always contain a cemetery, surrounding the church, an ossuary and a calvary inside an enclosing wall. Even in quite small villages, these enclosures are often surprisingly large and lavishly ornamented.

Off the coast of the Abers, the islands of the Ouessant Archipelago are scattered over the Iroise Sea, feared by sailors because of its reefs and dangerous currents. The winds here are so violent that only a few

Rochefort-en-Terre

To the south of the moors of Lanvaux, Rochefort-en-Terre crowns a hill, encircled by the vestiges of its ramparts. The village has a castle, several times rebuilt, an old covered market and a few Renaissance houses. But more charming than the monuments are the old wells, the humble calvary in the church and a wealth of enchanting details appearing around the corners of its flower-decked streets.

islands to become villages. The canals are no longer the only thoroughfares, but the Brière region is still best explored by boat. The island of Fedrun, the administrative center of the Brière nature reserve, still has many of its thatched-roof, whitewashed houses lining a labyrinth of canals.

Nantes is today the capital of the Loire country, but it was for centuries linked to the history of Brittany, and, alternating with Rennes, it was the seat of the dukes of Brittany. In the Retz region, the houses of Pornic climb the side of a hill overlooking the bay of Bourgneuf. The southern end of the bay is closed off by the island of Noirmoutier, which belongs to the Vendée region and is connected to the continent by a bridge over a narrow strait. This is a country of salt marshes, pine trees and mimosa, beaches and small ports.

Saint-Jean-de-Monts, Saint-Gilles-Croix-de-Vie and Les Sables-d'Olonne offer long, sandy beaches. Offshore, the island of Yeu was once occupied by Bretons who gave some of its places names that begin with "Ker," the Gaelic name for a house. Port-Joinville, where Marshal Pétain was imprisoned at the end of his life, has a long tradition of fishing for tuna. To the west, the Grand-Phare provides a magnificent view of the "Côte sauvage" and its jagged shale formations.

A little to the north of Fontenay-le-Comte, stands the church of Vouvant. We are approaching Anjou, "a province that seems to have acquired from its former masters a taste for things Italian," said the writer Flaubert. This province inspired the poet du Bellay, who was born in the castle of la Turmelière, near Liré, to write the famous lines:

> *"Plus que le marbre dur me plaît l'ardoise fine,*
> *Plus mon petit Liré que le mont Palatin,*
> *Et plus que l'air marin la douceur angevine."*

(To the hard marble I prefer the slender slate, to the Palatine hill, my little Liré. And to the sea air, the mildness of Anjou.")

Anjou assures a gentle life among its vineyards, its orchards, its gardens nestling on a hillside above a stream, in an enchanting landscape where a cypress sometimes adds a Mediterranean fragrance. In Angers the old streets with their Renaissance houses crowd close to the banks of the River Maine. To the south, Saint-Florent-le Vieil and Montjean-sur-Loire also have beautiful old quarters, clinging to the hillsides along the river. Farther on, Saumur is as renowned for its wines as for its equestrian and cavalry school.

Sein

Floating on the water, off the point of Raz, the island of Sein is separated from the continent by one of the most dangerous channels in France. According to legend, the little island was in old times the burial place of the druids. The hazards of landing, the naked earth devoid of all vegetation, and the tidal waves that have several times swept over the island may be at the origin of this story. When the lighthouse at Ar Men was built, at the end of the 19th century, to signal the long line of reefs in the approaches to Sein, it took around thirty years to finish the work because it was continually interrupted by violent storms. This view of the harbor is, however, hardly a turbulent one. Nevertheless, beneath their slate-covered roofs, the granite houses – often whitewashed, sometimes painted in vivid colors – huddle along narrow streets to fend off the ever-present wind.

In Montreuil-Bellay, a tributary of the Loire, the Thouet, flows below the old city and its castle. A short distance away, Fontevrault shelters the recumbent statues of the Plantagenets, among them that of Eleanor of Aquitaine, who came here at the end of her eventful life. The abbey, founded in the 11th century, had the particular distinction of being presided over by an abbess who was the head of both the men's and the women's community. One of the abbesses was the sister of Madame de Montespan.

Between Angers and Laval, the Mayenne Valley is dotted with villages, manor-houses and castles, perched on the hilltops with lovely views of, for example, Jaille-Yvon and Daon. Château-Gontier was founded by Foulques Nerra, a bellicose lord who inflicted harsh corporal punishment on himself and covered the region with buildings in an attempt to make amends for his sins. In Trappe-du-Port-du-Salut, the famous namesake cheese was for a long time made by the monks.

Laval, with its soaring steeples and towers surrounding its medieval castle was, during the French Revolution, a center of royalist dissent. Ambroise Paré, the surgeon to Henri II and his sons, was born in the vicinity. This was also home to the painter Douanier Rousseau and the writer Alfred Jarry, who created *Ubu*. On the wooded banks of the River Erve, the caves at Saulges, on the border with the Sarthe region, were inhabited in prehistoric times. A bit further south, the village of Asnières, on the banks of the Vègre, is built around an old mill, a 17th century castle and a church with beautiful wall paintings. The abbey of Solesmes, on the River Sarthe, was founded in the 11th century by Geoffroy de Sablé. The Benedictine fathers of Solesmes have, during the last decades, greatly contributed to the revival of Gregorian chants. The villages of Percé, Malicorne, Noyen and many others – strung out along the Sarthe, at the water's edge – possess ancient buildings that greet the visitor at the turn of a street. Old wells, churches adorned with touching sculptures and façades decorated with tiny turrets add to the charm.

Beyond Le Mans and its old town, where the writer Scarron lived, there is Pont-de-Gennes picturesquely situated on the banks of the Huisne. Saint-Calais, centered around its church, which has an Italian façade, has kept its old wash houses along the embankments of the Anille. Before it enters the region of Vendôme, the Loir River flows through verdant hills and valleys sheltering charming villages, manorhouses, churches and castles.

Vouvant

Vouvant lies protected by its ramparts, between fields and forests in the bend of a small river, the Mère. Its delightful setting, a beautiful Romanesque church and narrow streets lined with whitewashed houses have made it renowned as one of the loveliest villages in France. It is said that Vouvant owes its castle, of which only one tower subsists today, to the magic spells of the fairy Mélusine whose story lives on in the Poitou region. She is also said to have built, in a single night, the castles of Tiffauges, that recalls the sinister Gilles de Rais, as well as that of Pouzauges which also belonged to him.

CENTRAL FRANCE POITOU-CHARENTES

From the Beauce Plains in the north, through the Berry region, dotted with lakes and woods, down to the region of Tours, a country of chalk and vineyards, the region of the Center – including the magnificent Loire châteaus – also contains a number of charming villages.

In Illiers-Combray, the house of Aunt Léonie, dear to Proust, is today a museum devoted to the writer. Cloyes, also on the Loir, inspired Emile Zola when he wrote his novel *The Earth*.

On the banks of the Berry Canal, the castle of Mehun-sur-Yèvre belonged to Jean de Berry, who ordered from the brothers Limbourg the illuminated *Book of Hours, Les Très Riches Heures du Duc de Berry*. South of Bourges, the castle of Meillant has withstood the ravages of time, like the one at Ainay-le-Vieil – beautifully decorated during the Renaissance – and the more fortresslike Culan.

The moors and forests of the Sologne region recall "the country that can only be seen by pulling aside the branches," as it is described in *The Great Meaulnes*, by Alain Fournier, born in La Chapelle-d'Angillon, and in *Raboliot* by Maurice Genevoix, who was half Solognese. The old houses here are built of bricks, often laid in decorative patterns, or half-timbered, with cob filling the spaces in-between.

South of Bourges – where Jacques Coeur built his palace when he was finance minister to Charles VII – nestles the tiny village of Apremont-sur-Allier. It was completely restored at the beginning of this century. A castle, several times rebuilt, and a flower garden add to the attraction of the blond stone houses.

Nohan is the village where George Sand spent her childhood and where she was visited by Chopin, Balzac and Dumas. The places that she described in her novels are scattered all over the Berry region: the castle of Saint-Chartier, the mill at Angibaud, Neuvy-Saint-Sépulcre and La Châtre, where the Black Valley Museum is devoted to her. She also figures in the museum of Gargilesse-Dampierre.

Souvigny-en-Sologne

In Sologne we are close to the center of France and this view of Souvigny seems a happy and timeless picture of rural France. Well-kept homes on each side of the main street, the protective shadow of a church spire, a pretty town hall, a café where people call each other by their first names: this nostalgic atmosphere belongs here but one must remember that Sologne is a privileged region, proud of its magnificent game-rich forests where the romantic figure of the Great Meaulnes still lingers.

The old houses in Gargilesse, surrounded by low walls covered in flowers, rise up on the banks of a river, enfolded by trees. The calm and the simplicity of this village charmed the woman who wrote, "I would rather have a nettle in my own country than a beautiful oak anywhere else." George Sand often stayed at the Villa Algira during the last twenty years of her life. She depicts this area in many of her novels, as in *The Handsome Men in Bois-Doré*. Claude Monet and Théodore Rousseau, as well as other painters, came here to seek inspiration.

Close by, Saint-Benoît-du-Sault was the site of a Benedictine priory. The medieval village streets climbing up above the valley of the Portefeuille are still encircled by parts of the city wall.

Near the Loire, the sweetness of the Berry landscape is enhanced by the calm waters of the great river: "The wind is balmy without being sensual, the landscape is light, graceful but of a beauty that caresses without captivating, which, in one word, has more common sense than greatness and more wit than poetry: this is France," wrote Gustave Flaubert.

Not far from Chinon, encircled by vineyards, Candes leans against the limestone cliff where the first inhabitants took shelter. These ancient cliffdwellings have now been turned into woodsheds or cellars. The houses in Candes, just like the castles in the Loire Valley, have white stone walls built with the local tufa. The Romanesque church stands where Saint Martin, who evangelized the region, is said to have died. Because it is situated at the confluence of the rivers Loire and Vienne, Candes was formerly a busy port. In Lower Street, there are still houses where the bargemen used to live.

The writer Rabelais was born near Candes, at La Devinière. He invented the imaginary abbey of Thélème, on the banks of the Loire, a paradise whose motto was "Do what pleases you." Ronsard, who was born in the castle of la Poissonnière, sang the praises of his native Vendôme country in many of his poems.

All along the Loir, on the banks of lush greenery or white tufa cliffs, the villages have kept their medieval alleys and wonderful vestiges of past history. The remnants of the impressive towers of the castle of Lavardin rise above a classified village. In Montoire, the chapel of Saint-Gilles is decorated with magnificent frescoes, as are those of Saint-Jacques-des-Guérets and Areines. Other villages – for example, Troo and Les Roches-l'Evêque – still have houses cut into the soft rock of the cliffs.

"Leaving the jurists to the North, the troubadours to the South, Poitou is itself like its Mélusine, an assemblage of diverse natures, half woman, half serpent," wrote Michelet. Between the ocean and the heart of the country, the Poitou and the Charentes regions combine Romanesque churches and villages where cognac and goat cheese are produced; the ports, following in the wake of La Rochelle, retain their picturesque old towns, where Marennes oysters are served.

Poitiers, the capital, harbors many memories of its past. A few miles from the thoroughly modern Futuroscope, the old city of Poitiers is crowded with Roman vestiges, medieval alleys and a great number of churches, among which Notre-Dame-la-Grande is one of the finest examples of the Poitou Romanesque style.

In Lusignan, on the banks of the Vonne, a vast formal garden surrounds the castle of the lords of Lusignan. Although very little remains of their palace, their legend still haunts the area. The Lusignan family, some of whose members were kings of Jerusalem and Cyprus, is said to have resulted from the love between the fairy Mélusine and one of their ancestors. On the border between the Berry and Poitou regions, Angles is mirrored in the waters of the Anglin. The lower town reaches beyond an old stone bridge, toward the quarter of Sainte-Croix, while the upper town, crowned by tiles and slate, climbs up a hill to the plateau, watched over by the ruins of the castle. This was, in the 15th century, the home of Cardinal La Balue, secretary of state to Louis XI, who is suspected of having imported from Italy the terrible cages in which the king kept his prisoners and had them tried.

Candes-Saint-Martin

This very beautiful and very ancient village is built of tufa, the soft local stone which turns white as it ages. Here, one feels the sweetness of life in the Tours region, a country which is "ample and well-fed, rich to look at and in good health," as Flaubert put it. Saint Martin is said to have died in 397, on the spot where the Romanesque church stands (see the picture). His body was brought to Tours and, although it was the middle of winter, legend has it that the trees along the road sprang into leaf. This miracle gave rise to a pilgrimage which became very famous and attracted both kings and crowds of ordinary people.

This is also the home of the "openwork embroiderers" of Angles who embroider fine linen, tablecloths and napkins, formerly supplying the royal court and, later, the big ocean liners. A bit further north, Descartes has a museum devoted to the illustrious philosopher of the same name. The city was called The Hague before it changed its name to honor the man who lived for so long in Holland.

Saint-Savin, in the valley of the Gartempe, was in the old days the site of a powerful abbey. There remains only the abbey church, which is decorated with superb Romanesque wall paintings. Nearby, Chauvigny has the remnants of several castles, which, in the Middle Ages, defended this rocky spur on the banks of the Vienne. Chivray spans the two banks of the Charente and surrounds the Romanesque church of Saint-Nicolas with its lavishly carved façade.

In the Middle Ages, money was minted in Melle because of the silver-lead mines on the banks of the Béronne. As reminders of its past as an economic center, the city boasts three Romanesque churches.

Aulnay, in Saintonge, has a church whose front and inside capitals are adorned with beautiful sculptures. Beside the religious subjects, several animals are represented, among which is a donkey musician who reminds us that the "Poitou ass," a very hardy breed, contributed to the prosperity of the region until the 19th century. Villebois-Lavalette, in the southern part of the Angoulême region, was fortified by the Lusignan family. In the 17th century, the fortress was replaced by a castle which now dominates the village and its beautiful old houses topped by tiled roofs. A little to the south, in Aubeterre-sur-Dronne, many houses are cut into the

Here, one can already feel the soft air of the Atlantic coast and the islands. In summer, hollyhocks flourish in Saint-Sauvan, as they do in Talmont, stalwart on its peninsula overlooking the mouth of the River Gironde. The jewel of Talmont, the church of Sainte-Radegonde, is consecrated to the Frankish queen who founded an abbey near Poitiers. The beauty of the site, the white houses with their brightly colored shutters and the charming harbor make it one of the most delightful villages on the coast. The same type of houses can be seen farther north, at Mornac-sur-Seudre, where the workshops of the craftsmen and the multicolored shacks of the oyster-farmers lining the channels form an attractive picture. Mornac formerly made its livelihood from salt, like Brouage, which was the great local salt center in the 17th century. The walls raised to protect the city during the siege of La Rochelle have today been turned into a walkway from which one has a view of the islands of Aix and Oléron. Aix is a tiny island that can be reached only by boat. Everywhere, we are reminded that Napoleon spent his last free hours on this island before giving himself up to the English.

Eleanor of Aquitaine stayed for some time on the nearby island of Oléron before settling in Fontevrault, at the end of her life. This island belonged to the dukes of Aquitaine, but was coveted by both France and England. In the end, Richelieu built a citadel there. In Saint-Pierre-d'Oléron there are memories of Pierre Loti, a famous man born in Rochefort but buried here. The pine forests, the beaches and a climate warmed by the Gulf Stream, combine to make the island a popular holiday resort. Across the Antioche Strait from Oléron, also linked to the continent by a gigantic bridge, lies the island of Ré, "the white island," another bone of contention between the French and the English. This led to its capital, Saint-Martin, being fortified by Vauban in the 17th century. In a landscape of saltmarshes and oyster farms, the ports of La Flotte-en-Ré and Ars still have picturesque narrow streets.

North of La Rochelle, the Poitou marshes extend along the Sèvre Niortaise River, between the Vendée and the Deux-Sèvres regions. To the west, the "drained marshes" are used for farming and grazing. To the east, the wet marshes, called "green Venice," are crisscrossed by channels hidden among the trees, best explored in a skiff. The villages in the marshlands, such as Damvix and La Garette, gather their houses together on little islets with a boat tied up in front of the door. Only a few miles from Niort, there is a world where cars are almost unknown.

chalk of the cliff. Paved and flower-filled streets descend toward the river and to a 12th century church of a rare type: the monolithic church of Saint-Jean, built entirely in the hollowed-out rock.

"Angoulême is an old city, built at the top of a rock shaped like a sugar loaf… Nobody is ignorant of the fame of the paper mills in Angoulême" wrote Honoré de Balzac. Another old tradition is that of making cognac, which has been distilled in Charente for three centuries. The embankments of Cognac, the native city of Francis I, are lined with storehouses belonging to the major producers. Saint-Sauvan, near Saintes, was a resting place for the pilgrims bound for Compostella in Spain, as were Saint-Jean-d'Angély and Aulnay. Perched high up on a rocky peak, the village still has its fortified 12th century church and narrow alleys lined with low houses.

La Cotinière

The great diversity of the French landscape is one of its assets, but, strangely, in this region where nature does not indulge in any excesses either of landscape or climate, we find, side by side, the amiability of Souvigny, the exceptional artistic riches of Candes and the two faces of La Cotinière on the island of Oléron. La Cotinière is the most important shrimp-fishing port in France, but at the same time it is an easy-going tourist resort.

BURGUNDY FRANCHE-COMTÉ

Vézelay

When, in the 12ᵗʰ century, a monk laid out the itinerary recommended to pilgrims bound for Santiago-de-Compostella, the main stages in the south of France were Le Puy, Arles and Vézelay. Rising above a checkerboard of fields, the village of Vézelay, beneath its roofs of brown tiles, grew up around its immense basilica. When the future Saint Bernard came to preach the second crusade in the 12ᵗʰ century, Vézelay became one of the focal points of western Christianity. The basilica of Sainte-Madeleine was in a very poor state when Viollet-le-Duc undertook its restoration in 1840. The work lasted more than twenty years. The size and touching simplicity of the building with its long historical past and the charm of the steep narrow streets that lead up to it make this village in the Morvan region an experience that should not be missed.

Burgundy combines prosperous vineyards and meadows, where Charolais cattle graze, with secret fields and forests, limestone hills and valleys where peaceful streams flow. "France has no mediating element better suited to reconciling the North and the South," wrote Michelet. It is a fact that here, the gentle climate, the shape and the color of the roofs, sometimes decorated by tiles and Provençal friezes, already herald the South. In the Franche-Comté region both nature and climate are harsher. The slopes are steeper, the gorges, like those of the Doubs, are deeper, the forests thicker. The Jura is a mountainous region, with ski resorts, lakes and rushing water like the springs of Lison, the falls of the Doubs or the cascades of Hérisson. And as a true French region, Franche-Comté has its cheeses: Cancoillotte, Vacherin, Morbier and doubtless, the best-known of all, the Comté, produced for hundreds of years in local cooperatives.

History has, for centuries, linked these two provinces, so close but so very different. In the 9ᵗʰ century, Franche-Comté was called county of Burgundy, and although it had shown its independence by changing its name to Franche-Comté, it was still often joined to the Burgundy states through treaties and marriages, until the 15ᵗʰ century. Both of these territories have always been coveted, because they constituted the hub of the trade between the Mediterranean region and Germany, Italy, Switzerland and northern France.

The two regions also share a long tradition, that of the wine. Although the vineyards in the Jura are today much less extensive than those of "wine-rich Burgundy," their fame is still as great. In Burgundy, as in Franche-Comté, the historical sites and villages harbor treasures for both nature and art enthusiasts.

In the reign of Charles the Bold, the last Duke of Burgundy before Louis XI annexed the dukedom to the royal territory, Burgundy had extended its lands to include Franche-Comté but also part of Flanders and Holland. The power of the dukes of Burgundy and the prosperity of their lands are still visible. They allowed the Romanesque Burgundy art to flourish and to extend far beyond its place of birth. This influence accompanied that of the abbey of Cluny, which spread all over France and beyond, into Spain and Italy, from the 12ᵗʰ to the 14ᵗʰ century.

The size of the buildings, the delicate craftsmanship of the sculptures that graced them, their astonishingly expressive features, created a Cluny style that distinguishes the various buildings erected in the wake of the mother abbey. Among them are Paray-le-Monial, La Charité-sur-Loire and Vézelay, all superb examples of religious art. However, there are many less well known but

equally moving churches dotted around the Nièvre, Yonne, Côte-d'Or and Saône-et-Loire regions. Those of Charlieu, Chapaize and Ancy-le-Duc – and, in the vicinity, that of Semur-en-Brionnais, a village built of ocher stone and surrounded by vineyards – are remarkable examples of Romanesque art.

"Burgundy is the land of eloquence," wrote Michelet. Among the most eloquent was Saint Bernard, monk at Cîteaux – an abbey of great religious reknown – before becoming the first abbot of Clairvaux and, later, the spiritual guide who influenced popes and kings.

When he preached the second crusade in the presence of King Louis VII, at Vézelay in 1146, the abbey had already existed for three hundred years, but this event marked the beginning of its greatest flourishing. The abbey and the village crown a hill surrounded by fields and woods. To reach the basilica of Sainte-Madeleine, one walks up the steep streets lined with the former homes of local wine growers and beautiful houses with carved doors. At ground level they often have a row of windows lighting large underground halls, where, in old times, the crowds of pilgrims were accommodated.

Blanot

*Near Cluny, Blanot still has
one of the numerous priories
established under the impetus
of that great medieval abbey. Its
ancient houses have retained the
charm of the old villages in the
Mâcon region, surrounded by
vineyards and meadows. The prehistoric caves close-by deserve a
visit. The trail goes all the way
to Mount Saint-Romain, which
offers a wonderful view of the
countryside, the castle of Berzé
and Brancion, an old village ensconced between two narrow
gorges in a picturesque setting.*

The pilgrims of times gone by have been
replaced by the believers of today, who come to
worship at this spiritually still-powerful sanctuary,
and also by lovers of ancient monuments. The alleys
of Vézelay, with their old wells, small gardens and
occasional turrets have an air of serenity despite their
many visitors during spring and summer.

Another famous orator, Bossuet, was born in
Dijon, the former capital of the duchy. Montbard,
near the Cistercian abbey of Fontenay, was home to
two naturalists: Daubenton and Buffon. The former
created a park in the city and built a forge a few miles
away, where he conducted his experiments.

The Mâcon region has many memories of
Lamartine. The city where he was born has devoted
a museum to his life and work. In Milly, one can visit
his childhood home, which inspired him to write the
tender lines:

"Là mon cœur en tout lieu se retrouve lui-même!
Tout s'y souvient de moi, tout m'y connaît, tout m'aime!"

("There my heart feels at home everywhere.
There everything remembers me, everything knows me,
everything loves me.")

The castle at Saint-Pol, another tiny village
where he liked to stay, still looks the same as when the
poet lived there.

A list of all the famous Burgundians in love with their native land would be too long, but one must not forget Colette, born in the Puisaye region, at Saint-Sauveur, and the more recent writers Maurice Genevoix and Henri Vincenot. These three call to mind not only the love of words but equally the love of the fruits of the earth. What is more natural in a region where the mere names of cities and villages enchant all wine enthusiasts, whether neophytes or experts? The renowned côtes de Nuit and côtes de Beaune vineyards spread out between Gevrey-Chambertin, Vougeot, Vosne-Romanée, Nuits-Saint-Georges, Aloxe-Corton, Beaune, Pommard... These are all legendary names.

To this incomplete inventory must be added Chablis, further north, and the vineyards of the Mâcon region around Pouilly, Fuissé and Chasselas. Near these places, that radiate the "good life," the rock of Solutré, a curious 1,600 feet high plateau that dominates the checker-board of the vineyards. The panorama from its top is as breathtaking as its history. A museum down below shows archeological finds: it has been used as a hunting ground since prehistoric times.

Mailly-le-Château, Arcy-sur-Cure, Seignelay, Noyers-sur-Serein, Flavigny-sur-Ozerain... It is impossible to name all the delightful villages in Burgundy. Noyers, on the banks of a charming river, reveals a remarkable group of ancient buildings. The half-timbered walls and wood-carvings of the houses decorate the narrow streets that wind around the squares of the Marché-au-Blé or the Petite-Etape-aux-vins. Remnants of former ramparts still grace Flavigny and Noyers. Gargoyles adorn the medieval and Renaissance façades surrounding the ancient abbey of Flavigny. Former wine-grower's houses, erected on vast cellars, have been converted into farms since the disappearance of the vineyards.

The province of Franche-Comté stretches along the Swiss border all the way to the Rhône. It includes the Belfort territory, the Doubs, the Jura and the Haute-Saône regions. In Belfort, where the Vosges and the Jura meet, a natural depression – the "gap" – has often been used by invaders as an access route. The famous lion, sculpted in this rock by Bartholdi, symbolizes its resistance during the 1870 war. Besançon, the capital of the old Comté has a long tradition of watchmaking. Watches as well as the famous comtoise clocks have been made there since the 17th century. It is the birthplace of Charles Fourier, the creator of the workers' communes, and of the Lumière brothers, pioneers of photography and cinema. The architect Claude Nicolas Ledoux, after having imagined the "ideal city" of Arc-et-Senans, built, in Besançon, the first theater where everybody in the audience could sit down. Pasteur, born in Dole, spent his childhood in Arbois, where he returned regularly all through his life. Saint-Claude was the site of an important abbey during the Middle Ages and has, since the end of the 18th century, been the French pipe-making capital.

Lods, built on a hillside in the Loue Valley, which counts many charming villages, was for generations dedicated to growing the Poulsard, one of the most famous grapes in the Jura. The vineyards and the wine growers have disappeared from Lods but its steep alleys are still lined with greenhouses under roofs of flat tiles. A few miles away lies the charming village of Ornans, which has devoted a museum to its most famous son, Gustave Courbet.

Following pages
Baume-les-Messieurs

In the heart of the Jura region, Baume-les-Messieurs nestles on a verdant plain at the foot of a high cliff. The village grew up around an abbey founded in the 6th century by an Irish monk, Saint Colomban, who traveled through Burgundy before crossing the Alps to found other communities. In 1910, Monks from Baume-les-Moines established the abbey of Cluny. Baume-les-Moines was restored between the 12th and the 16th centuries by a rich Benedictine congregation which renamed it Baume-les-Messieurs. The buildings were transformed into homes during the Revolution and the cloister was demolished, but the church and some former monk cells recall the environment of the Benedictines.

A bit further south, almost on the Swiss border, Ferney was for twenty years the refuge of Voltaire. As a true "patriarch," he developed the small town, where he received numerous visits and wrote incessantly. Nowadays, the town calls itself Ferney-Voltaire.

It appears that there have been vineyards in the Jura region for at least five thousand years; at any rate, it is one of the oldest wine-growing areas in France, already mentioned by Pliny the Younger in the first century. Philippe the Fair introduced his wines to the court, and they were later much appreciated by such connoisseurs as Francis I, Henri IV and Rabelais, who praised their savor. Today the vineyards only cover a narrow strip of land between Arbois, Château-Chalon, l'Etoile and Saint-Amour. Yet, the yellow wine and the straw wine (which need years of maturing) or the red wines from Arbois are all the more appreciated by the experts. Thus, most villages in Franche-Comté have for many generations lived to the rhythm of the wine harvests. Many of the prettiest villages stand on the banks of the Ognon, the Lou and the Lison rivers. The vanished vineyards have been replaced by gardens or cherry orchards that delight the eye in the springtime.

Pesmes, to the north of the forest of Chaux, was once fortified in order to defend the western border of the Comté and it still has a few remnants of the ramparts. The alleys lined with flowers and houses with mullioned windows spin a web around a church of Romanesque origin on a plateau above the Ognon.

Lods rises from the hillside close to the source of the Loue, a small, winding tributary to the Doubs. The vineyards and the wine growers in Lods have all disappeared, but their sturdy houses, over vaulted cellars, can still be found along the steep streets. This is a peaceful village with its houses covered in greenery under flat-tiled roofs, its flower-lined streets and old fountains, grouped around a church with a slim spire. It no longer produces wine, but it has a museum devoted to wine and wine growing. A picturesque stone bridge spans the river, which is a paradise for trout-fishing enthusiasts. The Loue, its meandering course, waterfalls and lush green valley have often inspired artists, among whom is one of the greatest realist painters: Gustave Courbet, born in Ornans into a family of wine growers. He drew and painted his native country incessantly and often returned there until he was exiled to Switzerland after his unfortunate involvement in the

"Commune" during the war of 1870. In the *Funeral at Ornans* Courbet portrayed fifty inhabitants of the town, but the landscape and the people from his native region figure in many other works, such as, *The Castle of Ornans, The Source of the Loue* and *Women Sifting Wheat*. The house where he was born has been turned into a museum where his work is shown. In Ornans there are several bridges over the Loue. Stately Renaissance or classical mansions, small gardens, houses sometimes built on piles with a gallery opening out over the water compose an almost Venetian picture in the midst of the Jurassic Forest.

Starting from the banks of the Loue, Mouthier-Haute-Pierre climbs the sides of a hill in a particularly charming setting. A few remaining buildings from an old Benedictine priory have been restored and converted into homes. In Nozeroy, between the centuries-old fir trees in the forest of the Joux and the source of the Ain River, an old family of the Comté, the Chalon, had its domains. Their castle, which today lies in ruins, was the scene of sumptuous festivities for illustrious guests, among them Charles the Bold.

Near Château-Chalon, at the foot of a limestone cliff, more than 650 feet high, Baume-les Messieurs is sheltered under the trees on the banks of the River Seille. Like Baume-les-Dames, farther north, it is said to take its name from a Celtic word meaning "cave." In the rock of the cirque of Baume there are indeed caves whose rooms, festooned with beautiful stalactites, sometimes reach a height of 260 feet. The tiny village huddled around its church tower grew out of an abbey founded in the 6th century by a monk from Ireland, Saint Colomban. A few centuries later, twelve monks left Baume-les-Moines to establish the abbey of Cluny. The restoration of the original abbey of the humble monks of Baume was undertaken in the 12th century by a rich congregation of Benedictines and renamed Baume-les-Messieurs. The abbey church still harbors the tomb of Jean de Watteville, Abbot of Baume in the 17th century. The escapades of this soldier who became a monk are worthy of a cloak-and-dagger novel. He was forced to flee from France after a duel and is said to have taken refuge in Constantinople. He became governor of the Peloponnese and there obtained the title of abbot of Baume due to some unspecified skullduggery. Whether it is legend or reality, this story shows the importance of the abbey at the time.

AUVERGNE LIMOUSIN

The only volcanic region in France, Auvergne, was created by two geologic upheavals. To the ancient volcanoes, worn down by erosion, were added peaks separated by plains, formed later at the same time as the Alps and the Pyrénées.

To the south of Clermont-Ferrand, the range of the Puys can reach an altitude of over a 3,200 feet. It is a country for skiers; Super-Besse, for example, is an area of chalets and mountain hamlets that traditionally make their living from animal farming and milk products. To the north, the hills slowly decrease in height toward the border with the Allier region. Around Saint-Pourçain, there are fertile fields and vineyards. The Saint-Pourçain, which is both a wine and a cheese, is typical of the long list of specialist foods produced in the Auvergne: cheeses such as Saint-Nectaire, Fourme d'Ambert, Cantal, Bleu d'Auvergne, Murol, to name but a few. Other place names are coupled with traditional crafts practiced in the region for hundreds of years, for instance, Thiers and cutlery or Velay and lace. The volcanic nature of the soil has given Auvergne innumerable springs with various therapeutic virtues, depending on the rocks that the water flows through. There are numerous spas in the region: Vichy, Châtelguyon, Le Mont-Dore, La Bourboule. Chaudes-Aigues, as suggested by its name, has the hottest springs.

Passing through the Allier, Puy-de-Dôme, Cantal and Haute-Loire regions one finds alternately open villages, like Condat, and fortified ones, such as Auzon, generally perched on top of a hill. Many have used the characteristic dark stone for their houses, as the volcanoes that shaped Auvergne have also given it a building material that is unknown elsewhere in France: volcanic lava. Salers, built around the castle of the counts of Salers, was obliged to protect itself with ramparts to withstand the English and the large armies, idle after the end of the Hundred Years war, who ravaged the country.

Turenne

South of Brives-la-Gaillarde, the slate roofs of Turenne climb the hill below the imposing remnants of the castle of La Tour d'Auvergne. This family boasts two of the outstanding figures in Huguenot history: the Duke of Bouillon under Henry IV and his son, the great Turenne, who allied himself to Louis XIV after having participated in the Fronde insurgency. Formerly the seat of a viscountcy, Turenne has conserved the Salt Storehouse which was the meeting place of the States General, and many 15th and 16th century buildings, often decorated with turrets.

A part of the defensive wall erected in the 15th century still stands. The elegant mansions surrounding the Grand-Place are adorned with turrets, mullioned windows and carved doors, and they date from the Renaissance, when wealthy burghers settled there after it had become the bailiwick of the Hautes-Montagnes of Auvergne in the

16th century. Near the central fountain, a statue of Tyssandier-d'Escous reminds us that by improving the breed of red cows in the 19th century, he contributed to the reputation and prosperity of the city. The church, with its Romanesque portal, contains magnificent tapestries from Aubusson, the Limousin capital of this art since the 15th century.

At an altitude of 3,000 feet, in this "cold country under an already Mediterranean sky where one freezes on the lava," according to Michelet, snow often covers the pastures in winter. Usson, also built on a hillock, to the east of Issoire, displays the same black basalt color, but its roofs are tiled. It was one of the fortresses of Lower

Auvergne whose castle was said to be impregnable. Indeed, one of the city gates carries the inscription: "Fear only the traitor and hunger." In the lower part of the town, the old houses have often belonged to wine growers because, for a long time, Usson earned its living from wine before turning to animal farming and growing crops. The narrow streets climb up to the Romanesque church and then to the remnants of the castle, which was dismantled on the orders of Richelieu at the beginning of the 17th century. This castle had been host to Marguerite of Valois, the unruly Queen Margot, who, exiled from court by her brother, Henri III, was confined here for almost twenty years. Her imprisonment did not, however, prevent the willful queen from organizing memorable festivities.

Auvergne is richly endowed with Romanesque art, for example, the church of Saint-Austremoine d'Issoire, one of the largest and most noteworthy. Then there are the more humble ones such as the churches of Saint-Menoux, Saint-Saturnin and Arlempdes. The church in Ebreuil, on the banks of the Sioule, is decorated with precious medieval frescoes. That of Orcival, in the Monts-Dore mountains, was founded by the monks of La Chaise-Dieu, which was an important religious center in the Middle Ages. Its influence is partly explained by the fact that one of its monks became pope under the name of Clement VI. At Souvigny the Romanesque and the Gothic styles are both represented in the church of Saint-Pierre-et-Saint-Paul. This was the first priory created by the abbey of Cluny, in the 10th century, on land obtained from an ancestor of the Bourbons, Aymar, lieutenant to the duke of Aquitaine. The cathedral in Moulin, the capital of the Bourbon region, is in the flamboyant Gothic style and harbors a masterpiece of 15th century painting, a triptych in honor of "the master of Moulin," Pierre de Bourbon.

The orientally inspired cathedral of Puy-en-Velay has some exceptional religious art, but the most astonishing sight in the region is, without doubt, the chapel of Saint-Michel-d'Aiguilhe, perched on a lava peak behind the town. Another lava needle in the vicinity, the Corneille Rock, supports a gigantic cast-iron statue of Notre-Dame-de-France, erected during the reign of Napoleon III. The capital of Auvergne, Clermont-Ferrand, is dominated by the spires of a Gothic cathedral whose black stone is illuminated by magnificent, predominantly red and blue stained-glass windows. From another era, the basilica of Notre-Dame-du-Port is one of the most beautiful examples of Romanesque art in Auvergne. In its crypt, a black Virgin has been revered for centuries. Among its illustrious sons Clermont-Ferrand counts Blaise Pascal, while Teilhard de Chardin was born a few miles away in the castle of Sarcenat.

The castles in Auvergne are as varied as its landscape. The village of Murol, between the Mont-Dore and Saint-Nectaire, is crowned by the ruins of a fortress where today historical pageants are given. Another medieval castle is Chouvigny, situated above awe-inspiring gorges. It belonged to the La Fayette family, that of the famous general who was born in the castle of Chavaniac-Lafayette. The castle of Lapalisse was rebuilt during the Renaissance by Florentine architects.

In Châteldon, east of Vichy, in the foothills of the Bourbon Mountains, the vineyards have disappeared but the houses with wooden balconies, built by the wine growers, are still there side by side with beautiful medieval buildings. Some way to the north, Châtel-Montagne has an inspiring Romanesque church, while the Benedictine priory, built in the 12th century, is no more.

Salers

Salers is one of the villages in Haute-Auvergne that are built of volcanic rock and whose roofs are covered with stone tiles. Its houses, huddling around the castle, are austere –they are made to withstand the rigors of winter– but are gracefully endowed with all the decorative elements of Renaissance architecture: turets, pepper-pot towers and mullioned windows. Already during the Middle Ages, this was a prosperous city, renowned for a particular breed of cattle, to which it has given its name, as well as for its delicious cheese, the Cantal.

Following pages

Collonges-la-Rouge

The red sandstone houses of Collonge are framed by vineyards, walnut and chestnut trees. Its mansions and small castles, dating from the Renaissance, were the homes of officials serving the viscounty of Turenne in the 15th and 16th century. This charming village had a defensive role during the Wars of Religion which is recalled by the massive square tower of its church.

The high pepper-pot towers of the castle of Val, near Bort-les-Orgues, rise up from an islet in the middle of a lake. Its undisturbed exterior and its charming setting have inspired film makers, who have chosen it to stage cloak-and-dagger films. Also from the 15th century, the castle of Anjony, built of red basalt, looks down on the valley of the Doire. The castle of Effiat was constructed in the 17th century by the father of Cinq-Mars, who was a favorite of Louis XIII but was executed for having plotted against Richelieu. The story is told in the halls of this beautiful classical castle. The one at Parentignat, near Issoire, stands in an English-style park and dates from the beginning of the 18th century.

It is impossible to leave Auvergne without mentioning Henri Pourrat, who wrote *Gaspard of the Mountains* and was born in Ambert. He was a friend of Alexandre Vialatte, translator of Kafka, author and chronicler. He was originally from Limousin but spent a great deal of his life in Ambert and sang the praises of Auvergne in many of his works. Ambert also has pride of place in the book by Jules Romain, *The Mates*.

Between Gartempe and Vienne, and the rivers Dordogne and Vézère, the northern part of the Limousin region is a landscape of enclosed fields and deep valleys. To the west, along the border with the region of Charentes, it turns into pasture land, whereas to the south, toward Périgord, the climate becomes milder and walnut trees, corn fields, truffle farms and geese-breeding take over. In the east, along the border with Auvergne, the plateau of Millevaches is a country of moors and springs.

The emblem of the Limousin region is a leaf of the sweet chestnut tree. Up until the 19th century, immense chestnut forests provided the basic food for its inhabitants, as well as wood products, particularly staves for making barrels. From the end of the Middle Ages – when the devastation wrought by the Hundred Years War had to be repaired and the cities began to flourish again – the Creuse region provided all of France with workmen skilled in the building crafts. Since the opportunities were limited in the region of Limousin, its masons spread out to all the large urban centers. In the vicinity of Limoges, at Saint-Yrieix-la-Perche, deposits of kaolin were discovered in the 18th century. This raw material gave rise to a great local tradition: the manufacture of porcelain. Soon, large plants were built in the capital, Limoges, and porcelain became the successor of the enamel work that had been its specialty since the Middle Ages. Renoir, born in Limoges, started here as a painter on porcelain.

Blesle

The amazing architectural wealth of Blesle is a testimony to its long history. It began with the wife of the count of Auvergne, Bernard II, nicknamed Plante-velue. The Countess Ermengarde founded a Benedictine abbey around 870 and this remote site became the center of intense activity. During the Renaissance, Blesle was a prosperous town and the abbey attained the rank of royal abbey. The ladies, who must have four generation of noble ancestors, were awarded the titles of abbess and countess, had a comfotrable income and enjoyed a relatively flexible lifestyle.

The Limousin region is studded with fortresses, reminders of the long rivalry between the dukes of Aquitaine and the French kings. The road named Richard the Lion-Hearted allows the visitor to discover many traces

of these violent times. On the border with the Haute-Vienne region, the fortress of Rochechouart today houses a collection of modern art. Its buildings are a harmonious mixture of various styles from the 13th to the 18th century.

Coussac-Bonneval raises its pepper-pot towers around an Italianate courtyard. In the 18th century, it belonged to an adventurous lord of Bonneval who ended up as pasha in Constantinople.

Some distance to the south, Ségur-le-Château was the birthplace of the viscounts of Limoges. Its ruins look down upon the winding streets of the village, lined with houses decorated with turrets, mullioned windows and ornate façades. The castle of Montbrun, true to its reputation of being impregnable, resisted the attacks of Richard the Lion-Hearted. Its square keep, which is the oldest building, surrounded by four round towers, is reflected in a mirror of water. Nearby stands the castle of Châlus. Since it is situated on the border between the Poitou and Haute-Vienne regions, it was of major strategic importance. It was during an attempt to capture it that Richard the Lion-Hearted, son of Eleanor of Aquitaine, was mortally wounded in 1199.

In the heart of the Corrèze region, Ventadour guards the ruins of another crucial medieval fortress. The keep, from the 13th century, has endured through the ages and crowns a rocky peak with a spectacular view. This castle was the scene of grim battles during the Hundred Years war, but its name recalls primarily the 12th century troubadour, Bernard de Ventadour. This minstrel of courtly love was obliged to live in exile to evade punishment by the lords enraged by his success with the ladies.

The Limoges region also counts some of the most important stages for the pilgrims on the road to Compostella. They usually stopped to pray at a monastery founded by a saint a few centuries earlier. One of these, Solignac, was created in the 7th century by Saint Eloi, the treasurer of King Dagobert. Saint-Léonard-de-Noblat still has a beautiful Romanesque church, erected on the site of the monastery of Saint Léonard, the patron saint of prisoners. In Saint-Germain-les-Belles, a hospital was built in the 14th century for the exclusive use of the pilgrims; its fortified church dates from the same period. Several of the most beautiful classified villages in France can be found in Limousin – for example, Treignac, Saint-Robert, Curemonte and Collonges-la-Rouge. On the banks of the Vézère, Treignac covers the slopes of a hillock surrounded by low vegetation. A bit further south, Saint-Robert has a Romanesque abbey church, a remnant of a Benedictine priory. Curemonte, on the border between the regions of Corrèze and Lot, nowadays almost abandoned, still has a surprising group of castles and churches, survivors from past centuries of prosperity. A few miles from Collonges-la-Rouge, the village of Turenne sits on top of a hillock and offers a wonderful view of the undulating green hills in the Massif Central and the Dordogne Valley.

Lavoûte-Chilhac

The village with its Benedictine abbey lies ensconced in the gorges of the Allier River surrounded by the fertile plain of Limagnes. Brioude, to the north of Lavoûte, boasts the largest Romanesque church in Auvergne. It is also one of the most beautiful. During the Middle Ages, it was an important center of pilgrimage.

The ruins of a castle rise above the village with its medieval houses of white limestone, the Foirail Square and the Salt House. The castle belonged to the La Tour d'Auvergne family, whose two most illustrious members were the Duke of Bouillon, one of the leaders of the Protestant Party in the reign of Henri IV, and his son,

Henri de la Tour d'Auvergne, who joined the ranks of Louis XIV after the Fronde Insurrection and became one of the king's most faithful marshals. Many other villages, although not listed, are no less charming, for example, Moutier-d'Ahun, built along one single street among green hills crossed by the Creuse River.

Some way to the north, Guéret was the birthplace of the writer Marcel Jouhandeau, who described it in acerbic terms under the name Chaminadour. Bellac, on the contrary, honors its son, Jean Giraudoux, with a monument. This writer and diplomat showed more affection for his homeland in his novel *Suzanne and the Lover of Peace*.

RHÔNE-ALPES

From the Loire to the Ardèche, the Rhône-Alpes region descends slowly, from the Alpine summits toward a Mediterranean landscape. "The river Rhône is the symbol of the country, its fetish, just as the Nile is that of Egypt," wrote Michelet. On its banks, at the point where it is joined by the Saône, the metropolis of Lyon has grown up. Lyon was the capital of Roman Gaul, and already at that time, its position at a natural crossroads, where five great Roman roads met, made it an important center. The hill, called Croix-Rousse, was the site of the Gallic city whereas, on the other bank of the Saône the Romans built their forum, theater and capitol on the slopes of the Fourvière. An early convert to Christianity, Lyon, prompted by its archbishops, undertook the construction of a number of churches and abbeys in the Middle Ages. The Renaissance was for Lyon a period of great expansion, recalled in the sonnets by the "Beautiful Ropemaker's Wife," Louise Labé and by Maurice Scève, considered a precursor of the seven 16th century poets, the Pléiade. It was also in Lyon that Rabelais published *Pantagruel* and *Gargantua*.

The silk industry helped to increase the prosperity of this city of traders. "During the terrible upheavals of the first centuries of the Middle Ages, this great ecclesiastical city opened its heart to crowds of refugees. These people had neither fields nor land, only their own hands and their Rhône; they became industrialists and merchants," wrote Michelet. The alleys of Croix-Rousse were then the domain of the weavers. This network of lanes and courtyards echoing with the noise of the looms was the starting point of the silk workers' revolt in 1831, when the new looms, invented by Jacquard, put their livelihood at risk. Today, this is one of the most picturesque parts of the old city, like the Saint-Jean quarter and the squares of Terreaux and Bellecourt. Lyon was also the cradle of cinema at the end of the 19th century, before the Lumière brothers presented their invention in Paris.

The gorges of the Loire River cut through a long plain outlined to the west by the mounts of Madeleine and Forez, to the east by those of the Beaujolais and Lyon regions, and to the south by Mount Pilat.

Saint-Julien

In the heart of the Beaujolais region, the steeple of Saint-Julien looks down on a landscape of vineyards, source of the wine, "the third river in the area". The physiologist Claude Bernard was born here at the beginning of the 19th century. His home is now a museum devoted to his research.

The capital of the Loire region, Saint-Etienne, started to develop because of the coal field nearby, which specialized in the manufacture of steel weapons. In 1885, the establishment of the French manufacture of weapons and cycles in Saint-Etienne became the economic driving force in the city, selling its wares through the famous "Manufrance" catalog, until it disappeared a hundred years later. Today the city has one of the most interesting museums of modern art in France. Roanne, to the north, turned toward the textile industry, and from its port on the Loire, its products were exported north through the Briare Canal. In the 18th century, work was carried out on the Loire to allow Roanne to export goods from Saint-Etienne as well.

The village of Ambierle nestles on a hill above Roanne, among vineyards that produce rosé wine, near Saint-Haon-le-Châtel, where some beautiful Renaissance houses can still be found. To the south, Saint-Maurice-sur-Loire climbs up from the banks of the river to a ruined medieval castle. Saint-Bonnet-le-Château, south of Mount Forez, is known for its special interest in the "game of boules." The village is built around a Gothic-style collegiate church next to some ancient houses. It was once fortified and from the remnants of its ramparts there is a beautiful view over the surrounding countryside. In Sainte-Croix-en-Jarez, between Saint-Etienne and Vienne, the buildings of a Carthusian monastery, sold during the Revolution, now house a miniature village. Inside the rectangular fortresslike walls, two courtyards linked by a passage are lined with houses and small gardens.

The Rhône River has given its name to the neighboring district, which extends to the northwest of Lyon. The Beaujolais region, along the Saône River, was planted with grapes already in Roman times. Here, the names of the villages are recognized by all wine enthusiasts: Juliénas, Fleurie, Brouilly and many others. Scattered among the vineyards on the hill slopes, the houses of the Beaujolais region, under their roofs of Roman tiles, are built of grayish stone in the north, while in the south, in "the country of golden stone," the limestone is ocher-colored. There are remnants of fortifications in some villages – for example, Charnay and Ternand.

To enter the village of Oingt one still has to pass through the Nizy Gate. The village houses, constructed over vast cellars, line the narrow streets that are sometimes reserved for pedestrians. One of

Pérouges

There are few towns with such a beautifully preserved heritage. The Market Square in the heart of the town, the street of the Rondes, which follows the circular outline of the ramparts, and the Rue des Princes, where the house of the Princes of Savoy is located, offer superb examples of medieval and Renaissance architecture. Some of the houses still have their stone stalls on the ground floor, where shopkeepers and craftsmen laid out their wares for sale in times gone by. The pebbled fronts decorated with half-timbered walls and bay windows along the cobbled streets of Pérouges have often been used in historical films. The famous grammarian Vaugelas was born here in 1585.

Hauteluce

The village houses crowd around one of the most beautiful onion-shaped steeples of the Beaufort region. Northeast of Albertville, Hauteluce has access to the ski slopes of the Saisies, a resort at an altitude of 5,200 feet, specializing in cross-country skiing.

the buildings, the Maison Commune, dates back to the 15th century. The church was formerly the chapel of a castle, now in ruins. From Oingt one can see the Tarare Mountains, where the village of Chamelet winds along the valley of the Azergue, pinpointed by the spire of its beautiful church tower with its glazed tiles. The streets, sometimes turning into stairs, lead to a 16th century covered market and a dungeon from the 15th century. Between the Saône and Ain rivers, the Dombes region displays its woods and lakes. Francis I made it into a principality which did not belong to the kingdom of France until 1762. Its former capital, Trévoux, built in a bend of the Saône, still carries the marks of its former glory. Among the lovely mansions near the 17th century Parliament Palace, one bears the name of la Grande Mademoiselle, Duchess of Montpensier and cousin of Louis XIV. Farther north, in Châtillon-sur-Chalaronne, pretty flower-covered houses line a peaceful river. In this village, Saint Vincent-de-Paul was once the parish priest.

Filmmakers have often chosen Pérouges as the setting for historical films. *The three musketeers* and *Monsieur Vincent*, among many others, were set in its remarkably well preserved winding, cobbled streets. Coiled up at the top of a hill between Dombes and Bresse, Pérouges is said to have been founded by Italian colonizers, even before the Romans arrived. The city was attacked by the lords of the Dauphin and coveted by the princes of Savoy. In the 17th century, when it had become French, Pérouges got rid of its fortifications. Only the Street of the Rondes, which ran along them, still suggests their existence together with two city gates. Many of the houses in Pérouges date back to the 15th and 16th centuries, a period when hemp was the main source of income for its inhabitants. Some of the houses were destroyed or abandoned in the 19th century, when industrial weaving decreased the number of weavers. At the beginning of the 20th century, the creation of the Committee of Old Pérouges (of which the mayor of Lyon, Edouard Herriot, was a member) resulted in the village being included in the list of protected sites.

The Bresse region, renowned both for its cheeses and the quality of its poultry, has very original farmhouses. Their roofs are four-sided and topped by high pinnacle-shaped Saracen chimneys. These chimneys were linked to fireplaces that did not stand against a wall but under a protective mantelpiece, in the middle of the room, surrounded by a sort of trench where the family gathered for warmth. There are some beautiful examples of these houses in the villages of Saint-Triviers-de-Courtes, Grandval and Vernoux.

In the Haute-Savoie region, from Chalais to Faucigny, the alpine foothills, cut by deep valleys, offer views of extraordinary beauty, all the way to Mont Blanc, in the central massif of the Alps, which is their highest point. The foothills have been inhabited since prehistoric times – Annecy, for example, on the shores of the lake of the same name, former capital of the county of Genevoix. The Cathedral of Saint-Pierre saw Saint François de Sales saying mass and the young Jean-Jacques Rousseau, fleeing from Geneva at the age of sixteen, meet Madame de Warens in Annecy before settling on her estate at Chambéry. In *The New Heloïse*, Rousseau describes the beauty of the mountains: "The horizon offers the eye more objects than it appears able to contain: in truth, this scene has, I do not know what, of magic, of the supernatural that enchants the spirit and the senses; one forgets everything, one no longer knows where one is." Like Thonon-les-Bains and Evian, important health resorts, Yvoire stands on the shores of Lake Geneva. The fortified village of Yvoire was a port for boatmen before being a tourist center. The soothing climate and the streets, squares and balconies covered with flowers make it a haven of peace. Abondance, a hiking and crosscountry ski resort, sheltered one of the first priories in the region, dating back to the first years of the 12th century. It later became an abbey. The cloister still harbors magnificent frescoes. Châtel, in the middle of alpine meadows, is encircled by high peaks, as is Samoëns, a pretty village at the foot of a Collegiate church from the 16th century. The houses of Sixt-Fer-à-Cheval, scattered along a stream fed by the glaciers, hide their tiled roofs under a high wooded cliff.

Hauteluce

When covered by its mantle of snow, Hauteluce is a paradise for skiers, but in summer, it becomes a haven for hikers as well as for devotees of Savoyard cheeses such as the Tome or the Beaufort.

Near Chamonix and the "mer de Glace," Argentières huddles around a church with an onion-shaped steeple, typical of alpine villages. In Thône, close to Annecy, a square lined with arcades and old houses and graced by a lovely fountain is tucked away in the heart of the village. Farther to the south, Talloires looks down on Lake Annecy in a beautiful setting chosen by the Benedictines a thousand years ago for one of their abbeys.

Savoy produces the renowned Beaufort cheese as well as the Reblochon and the Tome de Savoie. Beaufort-sur-Doron is the site of two ruined castles and a beautiful Baroque church. Hauteluce has one of the loveliest church towers in the Beaufort region. Conflans, near Albertville, at the confluence of the rivers Isère and Arly, was a commerical center in the 17th and 18th centuries and has kept, as reminders of its past, some beautiful houses and a remarkable Baroque church. The village, high up on a hill, later spread down into the plain but has kept its characteristic colorful façades and its streets and squares enlivened by sculpted fountains. Close to the Italian border, Bonneval-sur-Arc is situated on the boundaries of the Vanoise National Park, as are Bessans, with its superb Baroque sanctuaries, and Aussois, overlooking the valley of the Arc.

In a bend of the Isère River, Grenoble lies between the massifs of the Vercors and the Chartreuse and the Belledonne ranges. The painter Fantin-Latour and the writer Stendhal were born there. The latter depicts his youth in Grenoble in *The life of Henri Brulard*. This is an ancient university town which nowadays also has a center for international exchange, called Europol. A cablecar links the center of Grenoble to the fortress of la Bastille, high up on a peak, which can be reached on foot through the Gardens of the Dauphins by climbing its steep slopes. The houses with their bright-colored fronts lining the embankments of the Isère, the lovely Grenette Square and pedestrian streets bordered by old buildings, together with wide avenues offering views of the surrounding mountains, combine to make Grenoble a most attractive city.

To the north, the fort of Saint-Eynard offers a panorama of the region where the peaks of Mont Blanc stand out in the distance. Further on, the monastery of the Grande Chartreuse has kept watch since the 11th century, sheltered in the forest. This was the first monastery founded by Saint Bruno.

The name also became that of the religious order created on this isolated spot. In the 18th century, the monks of the Grande Chartreuse invented an elixir for medical purposes, which is still made by the Carthusians at Voiron – but nowadays it is taken for pleasure. More than a hundred plants and resins are said to compose this drink whose secret has never crossed the thresholds of the distilleries. The Vercors Massif, to the south, recalls one of the major "Maquis" of the French resistance

Montbrun-les-Bains

At the southern end of the Drôme region, the stocky houses of Montbrun are almost Provençal. They rise up from a hillside close to the limestone flanks of Mount Ventoux in an oasis of greenery. In the fall, the village holds a lavender fair.

70

movement during the Second World War. This limestone formation is crossed by deep gorges, riddled with caves and covered by a dense forest, and was for a long time only visited by shepherds. Today, it is known to all lovers of undisturbed nature and protected sites. Villard-de-Lans, a well-known summer and winter resort, stands near the gorges of the Bourne, a torrent that rushes through a breathtaking landscape all the way to Pont-en-Royans. This lovely village built on a rocky outcrop used to produce the frieze cloth for the Carthusians' robes. East of Grenoble, the Oisans Massif has three peaks rising to nearly 13,000 feet: the Ecrins, the Pelvoux and the Meije. This is, above all, the country of ski resorts such as Chamrousse, Les Deux-Alpes and L'Alpe-d'Huez. The village of La Grave nestles at the foot of the peaks and glaciers of the Meije. A few half-timbered houses still grace this village, where Balzac is said to have found the inspiration for his novel *A Country Doctor.*

After this country of high peaks, the Drôme region seems quite Mediterranean. North of Valence, in Hauterives, stands the peculiar Ideal Palace, conceived at the end of the 19th century by "Facteur Cheval". Stone by stone, the postman spent thirty years constructing his monument bristling with minarets and decorated with a myriad of carved details whose artless exuberance recalls the painters of the naïve school. Some twelve miles from Montélimar, Le Poët-Laval, "the mount in the valley," raises its flat-roofed limestone houses, sometimes flanked by round towers. This is the region where lavender, cypress hedges and other Mediterranean plants make their first appearence. In the Middle Ages, the Knights of the Order of Saint John established a residence here for its commander which brought prosperity to the city. Grignan, in the Tricastin region, is known for the frequent visits paid by Madame de Sévigné to her daughter, who lived there. Above the village stands a magnificent Renaissance castle with beautifully carved façades where the marchioness lived out her days. From its terrace, the panorama stretches all the way to Mount Ventoux and the range of the Alpilles. La-Garde-Adhémar also offers a charming view from the top of its cliff, crowned by a lovely Romanesque church with a lacework steeple. The paved streets lead to the ruins of a Renaissance castle and a botanical garden, fragrant with local aromatic plants. Among the shady streets of Saint-Paul-Trois-Châteaux there is a museum devoted to the treasure of the Tricastin region: the truffle. The southern part of the Drôme region has another gastronomic specialty, the olive, which has been grown here for over five thousand years. Around sixty municipalities, between Nyons and Buis-les-Baronniers, are today involved in the production of virgin olive oil. Nyons is a medieval village with steep streets and beautiful ocher stone. In February it organizes a big festival marking the end of the oil-making season.

The Ardèche region includes the former Vivarais, whose capital, Viviers, still has two beautiful mansions from the 16th and 17th centuries. Near Valence, to the north, the ruins of the castle of Crussol, are perched on top of a rocky spur. This forbidding peak offers a magnificent panorama. North of Privas, formerly a Protestant stronghold, Antraigues is also an eagle's nest like Balazuc, further south, whose houses, grouped around the castle and the Romanesque church, look down on the Ardèche River.

Le Poët-Laval

Still within the Drôme region, Le Poët-Laval has a somewhat austere look, inherited from its medieval past as a fortified city. It still has remnants of the house built for their Commander by the Knights of Saint John. The streets around it are narrow as a protection against the prevailing north wind, the Mistral, and joined by vaulted passages, decorated with medallions and carved lintels. These alleys were deserted in the last century but the village is now protected and revived by artisans attracted by the beauty of the site, which is near Montélimar.

The gorges of the Ardèche are today one of the most popular sites in the region. Hemmed in by deep gorges, the winding river sometimes becomes a torrent. Its rocky banks, visible from the corniche roads (or, if one is adventurous, from a kayak) reveal charming villages such as Vogüé, near Aubenas.

A little to the east, Alba-la-Romaine was a prosperous city in the reign of Augustus. Remnants of Gallo-Roman baths, a theater and a forum have been excavated. A new city was built in the Middle Ages, and many of its alleys and vaulted passages can still be seen. The material for some of the buildings, such as the massive castle that surmounts the village, was taken from the basalt in nearby volcanic formations. The village of Saint-Montan overlooks the gorges of Sainte-Baume in a sublime setting. The ancient citadel clings to the edge of a ravine and its houses spill down the slopes below a ruined fortress.

AQUITAINE

The region of Aquitaine is often identified with the country around Bordeaux, its capital, or with Guyenne, so called when it belonged to England, from the middle of the 13th to the middle of the 15th century. Today the Aquitaine region includes five administrative districts, which, although they share a common history, have very definite characteristics of their own. The Dordogne has all the charm of the Périgord region: valleys crossed by rivers watched over by castles; villages of golden stone crowned by brown roof tiles; truffles, foie gras and canned duck on which the region has, for generations, built its fame. The Lot-et-Garonne region, covered with orchards where the plum holds sway, also grows tobacco, cereals and early vegetables, sold in the markets of Agen, Marmande and Villeneuve-sur-Lot. To the north, the region of the Landes unrolls its long ribbon of sand and dunes on the verge of the pine forests before becoming more hilly in the south. The Gironde region displays its vineyards dotted with estates, where the most noble wines are produced. The region of the Pyrénées-Atlantiques stretches from Béarn to the Basque country, between undulating hills and high snow-covered peaks.

The Périgord region is itself a mosaic of different landscapes. To the north, Green Périgord – criss-crossed by the Dronne, the Auvézère and any number of small streams– is a land of trees and water. Around Périgueux, White Périgord has a mixture of limestone plateaus and meadow-covered valleys. To the east, near Sarlat, Black Périgord, through which the Dordogne and Vézère wind their way, bristles with rocky spurs. The country around Bergerac, is called Red Périgord because of the many vineyards. Like all the territories in the southwest, where the French and the English battled it out, the Dordogne region is dotted with fortified towns. The oldest, Villefranche-du-Périgord, was built by the French in 1250. The remparts have disappeared, but its square, lined with arcades, has a beautiful covered market, its roof held up by an imposing beam structure. Between the sturdy houses surrounding it, one can still see the open spaces intended to keep fire from spreading from one house to the other. The most recent fortification, Saint-Barthélemy, to the west, was erected by the English in 1316.

The English also built Saint-Aulaye, on the borders with the Saintonge region – Vergt and Beauregard, south of Périgueux, and Lalinde, east of Bergerac, along the Dordogne Rriver, and Molière, guarded by the powerful square tower of its church. Among the French fortified towns, Monpazier has kept its arcaded square in the heart of the perfectly rectangular old city. In the 16th century, this was a stronghold of the Croquants, a peasant revolt that spread to Limousin, Périgord and Quercy, and described by Eugène Leroy in his novel *Jacquou le Croquant*. The insurgent peasants, also turn up in Domme. This fortified city was made triangular to fit the shape of the plateau on which it stands, high above the Dordogne River and surrounded by fields and woods. The path running along the cliffs offers wonderful views of the country around them while from the city center –past the beautiful covered market with its wooden balcony– the road leads to the caves where the people sought refuge in times of unrest.

These fortified villages are not the only places in the Dordogne area that deserve a visit. Saint-Jean-de-Côle, near the castle of Puyguilhem, mirrors its beautiful buildings in the waters of the river: half-timbered houses, an old humpback bridge, a covered market next to a strange Romanesque-Byzantine church. Some way to the south, Brantôme curls around a bend in the Dronne River. Its abbey, extensively remodeled, is said to have been founded by Charlemagne in the 8th century. Its bell-tower from the 11th century is thought to be the oldest in France. A cave in the vicinity offers a curious sight: its walls have been entirely covered with sculptures portraying the scenes of the Last Judgement. Also on the banks of the Dronne, Bourdeilles huddles at the foot of the castle that belonged to Pierre de Bourdeille, author of memoirs from the 16th century, better known under the name of Brantôme. Saint-Léon-sur-Vézère crowds around the dungeon of its ancient castle. The valley of the Vézère, dotted with castles and villages clinging to its banks, hides some of the most important prehistoric sites. The caves of Lascaux, near the lovely village of Montignac, Les Eyzies-de-Tayac and Bara-Bahau are the most outstanding ones. In the chasm of Proumeyssac there are extraordinary limestone concretions.

Beynac

In the region of Périgord, the Dordogne Valley was a transitional zone between English and French influence during the Middle Ages. At the time, the high cliffs towering over the river, that seems so peaceful today, bristled with fortresses such as the castle of Beynac. The lords of Beynac, who favored the French, were, all through the Middle Ages, opposed to the Cazenac, lords of Castelnaud, who were for the English. The ruins of their stronghold can be seen on the opposite bank of the river. This village, nestling between the rock and the river has the beautiful ocher color of the local stone.

The battlements crowning the dungeon of the castle at Beynac look down on the Dordogne River from the rocky spur protecting the back of the village. The houses of La Roque-Gageac march along the Dordogne while the wooded cliff rising above the village supports its castle. In the neighborhood, the castle of Fénelon sheltered the childhood of the man who was to be the target of the wrath of Bossuet and Louis XIV by his adherence to the doctrine of quietism and free thinking when he was a tutor to the young Duke of Burgundy. The castle of Monbazillac raises its white towers in the midst of the vineyards that produce a famous sweet white wine. Bergerac, close by, recalls two well-known names: Edmond Rostand and the forceful and moving figure in his play *Cyrano de Bergerac*, who was modeled on the real 17th century author of *The comic history of the States and Empires of the Moon* of the same name.

The region of Agen was also studded with fortified villages, some of which today have lost their defensive features as, for example, Tournon-d'Agenais and Durance. At Puymirol, a village founded by Raymond VII, Count of Toulouse, the ramparts were dismantled during the reign of Louis XIII, whereas Vianne has kept a large part of its city walls. Monflaquin stands on top of a hill and counts among the numerous fortified towns built by Alphonse de Poitiers, the brother of Saint Louis, like Villeréal and Lavardac.

In the Armagnac region, Poudenas, a pretty village situated near a waterfall in the Gélise, was equipped with a fortress in the Middle Ages. Rebuilt during the Renaissance, it is today surrounded by a park of rare trees which adds its charm to the ancient buildings and the mill at the river's edge.

In the region of the Landes, pine trees were planted in the 19th century to halt the advance of the dunes along the Atlantic coast where long beaches swept by strong waves tempt the intrepid. Summer resorts and coastal lakes are scattered along the coast between Mimizan, Hossegor and Capbreton. The local tradition of bull running is kept alive in Mont-de-Marsan and Dax, a spa whose popularity goes back to Gallo-Roman times. Here again, English and French fortresses stand face to face. In Villeneuve-de-Marsan, capital of the Armagnac region, where the renowned brandy is made, the crenellated tower, next to its fortified church, is said to predate the building of the fortress. In Saint-Justin, the arcaded square, a defensive tower and an old church line a paved street recalling the medieval village, decorated here and there with a few mullioned windows.

"The Garonne River passes by old Toulouse, old Roman and Gothic Languedoc and, always growing, it spreads out like a sea in front of the sea, in front of Bordeaux," wrote Michelet. The deep Gironde estuary waters the Médoc region: Entre-Deux-Mers, between the Garonne and Dordogne rivers; Sauterne, which extends it southward and Saint-Emilion to the north are appellations whose reputations rival each other. Saint-Emilion is also a very charming village which spreads out around the market square inside its ramparts. It is said that grapes

Molières

Nothing in this view of the Périgord village suggests its turbulent past. The site belonged to the powerful abbey of Cadouin when a fortress was built there in the 13th century. However, the population did not increase and the Hundred Years War and the Wars of Religion decreased it even further when they raged through the area. Nestling in its verdant setting, Molières leads a quiet life today in the shadow of its imposing church tower.

were grown here before our era. One of the few under-ground churches in France, the Château-du-Roi, a collegiate church and cloisters which enhances the charm of its old streets. The Médoc region is dotted with prestigious estates, rising up among the vineyards, some of which open their cellars to the public: Château-Lafite, Château-Mouton-Rothschild, Château-Beychevelle, Château-Margaux, among others. And the village of Sauveterre-de-Guyenne, in the Entre-Deux-Mers region, leads back to the lines of the fortified villages.

The export of Bordeaux wines has always been the driving force of the economy in the region. The Avenue of the Quinconces and the beautiful buildings around the square of the Bourse remind us that the merchants of the city of Bordeaux owed part of their fortune to the trade with the West Indies in the 18th century. Around the Arcachon Basin, oyster farming has for centuries been the mainstay of the economy as, for example, in Andernos, Gujan-Mestras and Cap-Ferret.

The region of Bordeaux is not only one of wine and gastronomy but also that of literary achievements. Montaigne was born a few miles from Saint-Emilion and studied in Bordeaux. Toward the end of his life he retired to his estate of Montaigne and, for some ten years, worked on his *Essays*. Montesquieu, the author of *Persian Letters* and *The Spirit of Laws*, began his life in the castle of La Brède, south of Bordeaux. The writer François Mauriac was also born in Bordeaux.

South of the Adour River begins the region of the Pyrénées-Atlantiques. From Bayonne to Pau, from Bidache to the Somport Pass or to the Pourtalet Pass, the landscape and the villages show many facets, from the coast battered by the ocean to the undulating countryside and the high mountains. The "Euskadi," the Basque country, announces by its name its identity as a separate country. Ignoring the Pyrénées, it includes three regions in France (Labourd, Basse-Navarre and Soule) and four in Spain (Biscaya, Guipuzcoa, Alava

decorate most of the houses. These colors appear again in Bayonne, capital of the Labourd region, on the high narrow façades along the embankments of the Nive. Saint-Jean-de-Luz was, in 1660, the scene of the marriage between Louis XIV and the infanta of Spain, stipulated by the Treaty of the Pyrénées. Sheltered by a deep bay, this harbor has, over the centuries, been involved in every type of fishing: whaling, cod-, sardine- and tuna-fishing. Cibourne, the "bridgehead," facing Saint-Jean-de-Luz on the other bank of the Nives, is the birthplace of the composer Maurice Ravel. The beauty of the city and its surroundings, defended by Fort Socoa, has enchanted painters and writers – for example, Pierre Benoit, who spent the latter part of his life there. Hendaye stands on the banks of the Bidassoa that forms part of the frontier between France and Spain. The river holds the smallest shared territory in the world, the island of Les Faisans, governed in alternating six-month periods by the two countries. Inland, the houses in Espelette, capital of the red pepper, are, in the fall, festooned with strings of red fruit drying in the sun. Aïnhoa, close to the frontier post of Dancharia, was founded by the Premonstratensians as a staging post on the road to Santiago-de-Compostella. Its lovely half-timbered and whitewashed houses are sometimes decorated with wooden beams carrying an inscription or a date.

In the valley of the Joyeuse, La Bastide-Clairence has the same white houses with timber frames painted green and red. The capital of Lower-Navarre, Saint-Jean-Pied-de-Port, was the seat of the lords of Albret. Mirrored in the waters of the Nive, some of its houses have red sandstone fronts like that of the fortified church of Notre-Dame. Near the vineyards of Irouléguy, Saint-Etienne-de-Baïgorry stands in the valley of the Aldudes against the magnificent backdrop of the Pyrénées. The tiled roofs give way to slate in the region of Soule. This is mountain country with spectacular gorges such as Kakouetta and Holçarté. Mauléon, its capital, lies in the shadow of a fortress that towers above it; the town has for centuries been a center for the production of espadrilles and shoes. Larrau, surrounded by pastures, Sainte-Engrâce with its beautiful Romanesque church and Arette-Pierre-Saint-Martin, with its ski slopes are all set in the midst of magnificent scenery. So is Pau, the capital of the Béarn region, where Henri IV was born. It offers a wonderful panorama of the mountains and the soaring peak of Midi d'Ossau.

and Navarra). Divided by the vagaries of history between two kingdoms, the Basque Country has kept as its motto "Four plus three make one." The language, whose origin still bewilders the linguists, has remained the same on both sides of the border, just like the famous game of pelota, the traditional dances such as the fandango and the importance of the "etche," the house identified with the family, which is all-important. The two colors of the Basque flag, green and reddish brown, embellish the wooden panels that

Labastide-d'Armagnac

The rectangular square in Labastide-Armagnac, lined with beautifully wood-paneled arcades, is said to have inspired the architects of the Place des Vosges in Paris. Some of the houses surrounding the imposing fortified church still have their half-timbered fronts. Among all the fortified villages born of the rivalry between the French and the English in the 13th and 14th centuries, this one, to the east of Mont-de-Marsan, is one of the best preserved.

Following pages
Aïnhoa

Aïnhoa, the "Good Spring", is a typical one-street-village. In the old days, a staging post on the road to Santiago-de-Compostella, it was also an important center for trade between Bayonne and Pamplona. The whitewashed houses are decorated with wooden panels painted green or red, the colors of the Basque flag. The asymmetrical roofs, common in the Labourd region, protect the fronts of the houses from rain and dominant west winds; the disc-shaped gravestones in the cemetery, next to the church, are typical of the Basque Country.

MIDI-PYRÉNÉES

From north to south, the Midi-Pyrénées region includes eight administrative districts with very different landscapes, from the Lot Plateau to the Pyrénées –"the formidable barrier of Spain," as Michelet called them. Toulouse is the dynamic capital of the region.

The villages in the Lot region – with their golden stone, the isolated mansions, flanked by square towers and dovecotes – are enfolded by forests, vineyards and fields. Many have high roofs of brown tiles pierced by attic windows, typical of the region as in Carennac, a very beautiful classified village. Some way to the south, after the Padirac Chasm, Autoire fills a wooded cirque with a mixture of half-timbered houses and large buildings. Near Presque Cave, bristling with concretions, Saint-Céré surrounds the square of the Mercadial, lined with ancient houses that have kept their original character.

West of Gramat, Rocamadour seems to defy the laws of gravity. It presents the most striking picture as it climbs the steep slopes of the gorges of the Alzou to its basilica and chapels at the top. The village has been an important center of pilgrimage since the 12th century, when the miraculously preserved body of Saint Amadour was found on the spot where the chapel of Notre-Dame now stands. The worship of Notre-Dame of Rocamadour spread far and wide, and kings, saints and anonymous pilgrims came to pay homage to the black Virgin of the Saint-Sauveur basilica. During the crusade against the Albigenses, the heretics that were to be chastised had to mount the two hundred and sixteen steps leading from the village to sanctuaries on their knees. Devastated during the Hundred Years War and later by the Wars of Religion, Rocamadour was deserted for a long time until the bishops of Cahors undertook to restore it in the 19th century. Today it is one of the most visited places in the country.

Lacapelle-Marival, dominated by a stalwart castle, has a beautiful medieval old town. The houses of Espagnac-Sainte-Eulalie, in the valley of the Célé, form a picturesque group around a church with a curious tower built of wood and bricks topped by an eight-sided roof.

The banks of the Lot are dotted with villages where each alley hides some interesting detail: a fountain, a wash-house, a dovecote or a communal bread oven. Near Fumel, a road leads through the woods to Bonaguil, a tiny hamlet crowned by a fortified castle. Erected at a time when castles were only built for pleasure, this fortress with its boat-shaped keep, far from the great thoroughfares, has never had to defend itself from the slightest attack.

The fortress at Saint-Cirq-Lapopie has, on the contrary, often been an object of desire. It resisted Richard the Lion-Hearted but was dismantled by Louis XI three centuries later before being taken over by the Huguenots. The population, sheltering behind the walls in the Middle Ages, consisted mostly of craftsmen, in particular, wood turners. Recently, artists and successors to the former artisans have greatly contributed to the restoration of the houses – with their bay windows, balconies and small gardens – which line the paved streets.

In the Rouergue region, the River Lot continues its course through the Aveyron, its banks alive with villages that overhang spectacular gorges. Conques stands above the River Ouche, near its confluence with the Dourdou. Around the magnificent church of Sainte-Foy, part of a vanished Benedictine abbey that was very influential in the Middle Ages, a maze of steep streets cling to the hillside, interspersed with small squares lined with granite or shale houses in beautiful ocher colors. Entraygues-sur-Truyère, somewhat to the east, and Estaing, where a Gothic bridge spans the Lot, have also kept their enchanting old houses.

Saint-Cirq-Lapopie

The houses of the "pearl of Quercy" cling to a steep rock rising above the valley of the Lot river. Because of its strategic position, it was repeatedly attacked during the Hundred Years War and the Wars of Religion. Nevertheless, its rich artistic heritage was preserved and reflects five centuries of history. In the shadow of its massive church, the houses with their bay windows and flower-decked balconies now line peaceful paved streets, crowded with visitors every summer. Potters, weavers and painters have given new life to this village where the street names recall the artisans that used to work here, for example, rue Pelissaria (the furriers) or rue Peyroleria (the coppersmiths).

In the valley of the Dordogne River, Carennac became in the 10th century the site of a priory where Fénelon lived for fifteen years. Carennac enchanted him and he wrote of it: "This blissful corner of the world delights me and laughs in my eyes." It is included in the list established by the association for the most beautiful villages in France.

Following pages

Conques

High above the valley of the Ouche, Conques owes the size and the beauty of the church of Sainte-Foy to a Benedictine abbey, which, in the Middle Ages, became an important religious center. The church with its three towers in pure Romanesque style, today seems disproportionate to the little village in the middle of the forest, but in the past, Sainte-Foy welcomed the pilgrims walking to Compostella. It has one of the most precious gold and silver treasures, of which the most outstanding is a reliquary, a wooden statue covered with gold leaf and studded with precious stones, called "the Majesty of Sainte-Foy." The houses in Conques are built of granite or shale, occasionally with timber frames, or finished in an ocher wash. Their roofs are high and covered with stone tiles, sometimes slightly curved at the bottom. Not much has changed here since the Middle Ages.

In Estaing, the houses built of shale, sandstone and pebbles from the Lot, surround a Renaissance castle. On the border between the Aveyron and Lozère regions, Saint-Côme-d'Olt, a beautiful fortified village, is dominated by the spiral tower of its church. Sainte-Eulalie-d'Olt, close by, was formerly inhabited by weavers and tanners. Both villages owe much of their charm – and their names– to the River Lot, which used to be called "Olt."

South of Villefranche-de-Rouergue, Najac sprawls along a corniche high above the Averyron River. The ruins of its fortress and its Gothic church still vibrates with the memories of battles between Catholics and Cathars and French-English rivalries. Nevertheless, Najac has retained many of its 16th century houses. To the east, part of the Larzac Plateau was ceded to the order of the Templars in the 12th century, then to the Knights of Saint-John. They founded a fortified village, La Couvertoirade. Strong walls encircle houses with tiled or stone-covered roofs, built of the limestone of this arid country. Outside the walls, a small pond where the sheep drink reminds us that the village was formerly inhabited mostly by shepherds.

Albi, the capital of the Tarn region, with its imposing Gothic cathedral, Sainte-Cécile, built entirely of brick, and the palace of the Berbie, was in the 13th century the scene of bloody battles between the Catholics and the Cathars. At the beginning of the 13th century, the king of France took up arms against his powerful vassal Raimond VII. This count of Toulouse was accused of being sympathetic to the Cathar doctrine which had spread across his land. In 1209, the crusade against the Cathars was entrusted to Simon de Montfort, who abandoned the country to the pillage and massacres of his mercenaries until Raimond VII was utterly defeated at Muret in 1213. Monfort then proclaimed himself Count of Toulouse, but was assassinated in 1218. Raimond VII took back his title and, to protect his subjects, he decided to build a new fortress. He chose Cordes, perched on the rock of Mordagne, a few miles north of Albi. It later became a hunting residence for the lords of Languedoc and continued to grow until it became, during the Renaissance, a place of feasts and fairs where commerce prospered. Along the Grand-Rue, elegant houses grew up next to the old ones of brick and cob, along the steep winding streets of the village.

The rose-colored houses, windows adorned with pointed arches and small columns and balconies overlooking the street create an atmosphere reminiscent of Italy in the city of "a hundred arches." The old covered market in the heart of the village recalls the bustling market days of long ago. Locally made leather and fabrics were sold there as well as pastels and saffron produced in the region. Then, Cordes went to sleep for a long time. It was a painter, Yves Brayer, who caused its awakening in the 20th century.

He was followed by many artisans and artists who have reviv-ed the village whose lovely name is actually Cordes-in-the-Sky. South of Albi, Lautrec has always been a villa-ge of merchants, as can be deduced from the beautiful market square surrounded by houses with corbelled balconies supported by wooden pillars. Formerly, it was a fortified village overlooking the plain of Castres but, today, only a gate is left of the fortifications, erected in the Middle Ages; it has, for centuries, produced delicious pink garlic.

Gaillac stands on the River Tarn, in the midst of vineyards that produce a vast array of wines, in particular, renowned white wines. Some distance to the north, Puycelci seems to be floating on the forest of Grésigne. The fortress, built on a plateau, emerges from the trees, encircled by ramparts protecting its 15th and 16th century houses. Penne, another medieval stronghold, towers over the Aveyron on a rocky peak that offers a splendid view of the surrounding country.

Nearby, in the Tarn-et-Garonne region, the ancient houses of Bruniquel crowd around a castle that, according to legend, was built by Brunehaut, the daughter of a Visigoth king, who became queen of the Eastern kingdom, Austrasia. Saint-Antonin-Noble-Val combines medieval and 18th century houses with a rare 12th century building converted into a museum. The same narrow streets weave the village of Caylus, on the banks of a tributary to the Aveyron, in the pretty valley of the Bonnette. Montauban, native village of the painter Ingres, has devoted a museum to him in the former episcopal palace, built of the local brick that gives its warm color to this part of the southwest. This walled city was declared a safe haven for protestants in 1570. In the surrounding area, other fortified villages have medieval streets laid out around an old covered market, for example Puylaroque nestling on top of a hill, Montpezat-de-Quercy and its splendid square lined with arcades, Lauzerte perched on a rocky spur, Auvillar with its port on the Garonne River and Caussade, which has become an important center for the manufacture of hats.

Surrounded by hills where sweet-flavored chasselas grapes are grown, Moissac boasts one of the most outstanding examples of Romanesque art in France: the Abbey of Moissac. In the 11th century it became attached to Cluny and gained considerable influence throughout the southwest. The church of Saint-Pierre bears witness to its former power. The southern portal is a masterpiece of Romanesque art as is the adjoining cloister with its harmonious proportions and seventy-six arcades decorated with exquisitely carved capitals.

In the Armagnac region, fortified villages grew up all through the 13th century, until the middle of the 14th, according to political and economic needs – among others, those of the rivalries between the French and the English, caused by the marriage of Eleanor of Aquitaine to the English King Henry II. Between Mont-de-Marsan in Aquitaine territory and Auch, the capital of the Gers region, the two warring parties built fortifications around the cities on the roads leading from the Toulouse region to Guyenne.

To the east, Saint-Clar-l'Anglaise stands between Miradoux, Fleurance and Montfort, built by the French. To the north, the English erected the completely circular Fourcès which faces Montréal, rectangular in shape and one of the oldest villages fortified by the French as well as one of the most beautiful. To the west, toward the Guyenne, the narrow front line has put the English villages Mauvezin, Labastide-d'Armagnac, Saint-Gein, Monguilhem and Lias next to the French ones: Saint-Justin, Monclar, Villeneuve-de-Marsan, Rondeboeuf and Maguestau.

To the south, there are innumerable, although less tightly spaced, French constructions: Plaisance, Bassoues, Marciac, Miélan, Mirande, Pavie, Aujan, Villefranche, Cologne… All these villages, hiding behind their defensive walls, have kept their medieval character. Around beautiful covered markets, lined with arcades that protected humans and goods from the weather, the alleys are bordered by superb half-timbered houses and defensive-looking churches, often flanked by an eight-sided tower.

The region of the Hautes-Pyrénées calls up visions of peaks, passes, torrents and lakes, a preserved natural environment, such as can be seen in the Néouvielle Nature Reserve. Close to the Spanish border, the cirque of Gavarnie is one of the spectacular sights that have inspired many artists. "The most beautiful sight that I have seen," wrote Flaubert. Lourdes is known all over the world for its pilgrimages, but there are also small spas and villages that deserve a visit in this area.

Argelès-Gazost still has among its steep-roofed chalets a casino and handsome buildings that were built in the 19th century for the enjoyment of the people drinking the curative waters. Nearby, Saint-Savin has a remarkable Romanesque church and a magnificent view over the surrounding country from a

Cordes

In the 13th century, King Philippe Auguste entrusted Simon de Montfort with the task of eradicating the Cathar doctrine, considered by the Catholic church to be heretic, which had spread across the territories of the count of Toulouse. Raimond VII, seeing the pillage and massacres perpetrated by Monfort's mercenaries, decided to build a new fortified city to protect his subjects: he founded Cordes, a few miles north of Albi. The city prospered during the Renaissance and was enriched by the elegant mansions that grace it today. After having been deserted for a long time, it was revived by artisans, lace makers, embroiderers, painters and sculptors who nowadays inhabit its lovely, steep, winding alleys.

terrace near the town square. Cauterets, whose waters are said to cure everything, stands on a superb site, surrounded by torrents, mountain paths and, in winter, ski trails.

Luz and Saint-Sauveur, the spa made famous by Empress Eugénie, who stayed there in the 19th century, and Barèges, where Madame de Maintenon came to take the waters in the 18th century, have the same views and the same activities. The ski slopes at Barèges are linked to those of La Mongie, the well-known ski resort in the Pyrénées, while, farther to the east, the chalets of Saint-Lary are scattered across the Valley of the Aure.

Arreau, the former capital of the Country-of-Four-Valleys (those of Aure, Barousse, Neste and Magnoac) is crossed by small torrents that run along its corbelled and half-timbered houses, one of which is the famous Maison du Lys with its Renaissance façade. The Romans mined the iron and copper deposits not far from the marble quarries of Campan and Sarrancolin.

The Haute-Garonne region, whose powerful center is Toulouse, was the capital of the Visigoths and has a rich historical heritage. The site of Saint-Bertrand-de-Comminges has one of the most peculiar pasts. It was founded in 72 B.C. by Pompeius and the city, nicknamed "the Mont-Saint-Michel on land," grew to have a population of 60,000 before it was almost abandoned, until the 12th century when the bishop of Comminges, the future Saint Bertrand, decided to build a cathedral there. The cathedral of Sainte-Marie was later enlarged by Pope Clement V and its magnificent wood panelling was carved by 16th century masters from Toulouse. It is flanked by a cloister whose arcades open out to give a view of the mountains. The village huddles beneath its massive shape on top of a hill, surrounded by fields, vineyards and cypresses. Outside the city walls, the vestiges of the Roman era extend over a wide area. The Episcopal Palace, erected by the bishops of Saint-Bertrand, is still the main feature of the hamlet of Alan. Further to the east, on the hills of Volvestre, the villages of Montesquieu and Rieux harbor old houses and churches. In Rieux, where two old bridges span the Arize, the eight-sided cathedral tower with lacework galleries is one of the most beautiful examples of the Toulouse style. Saint-Felix-Lauragais, towering over the plain, has a wealth of historical vestiges around its castle: sections of ramparts, a covered market from the 14th century, mills nowadays deprived of their working parts, and half-

timbered houses restored by the artisans that have revived the village. It is said that the first Cathar council was held here in 1167. Within the Midi-Pyrénées district, it is in the Ariège region, on the border of the province of Languedoc, that the most numerous and most impressive vestiges of the Cathars can be found. In the vicinity of Foix, the castles where they sheltered are innumerable.

Aurignac

The village stands out against the many-colored bakdrop of the Pyrénées. From the ruins of its medieval keep, the view of the surrounding country is breath-taking. However, it is not the beauty of its setting that has made the reputation of this hamlet in the Haute-Garonne region. A paleolithic period has been called the Aurignacian since bones and carved tools were unearthed here some time before their contemporary, the Cro-Magnon man, was found at Eyzies-de-Tayac in the Dordogne.

They often stand on a rocky outcrop, spectacular eagles' nests overlooking the roads, as, for example, Roquefixade, Lordat and Montségur, which symbolizes the end of the Cathars. In 1244, the last believers, having taken refuge in Montségur, were driven from their place of safety and brought to the stake, where they were all burned alive, taking with them the secret of a mysterious treasure which they were thought to have had time to hide. Mirepoix, another of their strongholds, has today beautiful half-timbered houses around a market square lined with arcades. The village was drowned at the end of the 13th century, when a dam burst in Lake Puivert, and rebuilt not far from the Hers, a small river that also flows past Camon. Legend has it that Charlemagne founded it.

LANGUEDOC ROUSSILLON

"It is a very old country, this Languedoc. You find everywhere ruins under the ruins; the Camisards (insurgent 18th century protestants) on top of the Albigeois (Cathars), the Saracens on top of the Goths, underneath them, the Romans, the Iberians," wrote Michelet. From the Roussillon region, that just about covers the Pyrénées-Orientales district, through the mountains of Aude, the plains of the Hérault and Gard regions to the Cévenne foothills in Lozère, a long history is written in stone. Here, the Romans, the Visigoths and the Saracens have all left marks of their culture. Later on, the frontier between France and Spain was for a long time undetermined, which made Catalonia a world somewhat apart with its own language and traditions. The Cathars as well as the Calvinists found support there. It may be that their rigorous doctrines suited this land, warmed by the Mediterranean sun but harsh and dry, whose beauty is more austere than graceful. Each of these regions has its own type of architecture: in the mountains, the roofs are covered with stone tiles; in the Causse region the houses are built of limestone; among the vineyards, they are different again. All have their own particular shape, color and charm.

A few miles from Spain, in a cirque of the upper Tech Valley, the village of Prats-de-Mollo huddles around the House of the kings of Aragon, near the square del Rey. The fortifications of the upper village, encircling beautiful medieval streets, were strengthened by Vauban in the 17th century. He also founded Mont-Louis after the treaty of the Pyrénées, by which Spain ceded Roussillon to France and divided Cerdagne between the two countries. The formidable fortress constructed at an altitude of 5,200 feet was never obliged to prove its strength, nor did Villefranche-de-Conflent, which is enclosed in a deep valley at the confluence of two rivers. This rectangular village already had a high defensive wall but it was reinforced by Vauban in the same period. This tight belt has

preserved the narrow streets lined with houses whose beauty is occasionally enhanced by mullioned windows and old shop signs. The façade of the church of Saint-Jacques –whose portal is made of the pink marble that can also be found in the small columns on some of the house fronts– together with the brick watchtowers add their touches of color to the enchanting picture. The "little yellow train" leaves from this village to meander through the Cerdagne region for the sole pleasure of the tourists.

La Roque-sur-Cèze

The Cèze, a small tributary to the Rhône, flows from the Cévennes Mountains through spectacular gorges upstream of La Roque. The village, dotted with the spires of cypresses, nestles around a beautiful Romanesque chapel on a hillock overlooking the river.

Two magnificent medieval abbeys stand close to the Canigou Mountain, which reaches a height of 9,800 feet. The Catalans consider it their "Mount Olympus." The churches of Saint-Martin-du-Canigou and Saint-Michel-de-Cuxa are both crowned by a crenellated square tower in a wonderful setting. In the foothills of the mountain, Castelnou looks down from a rocky peak encircled by 13th century ramparts. The alleys, lined by ocher-colored houses, are as steep as those of Eus – pronounced Eousse – near Prades. Here, the steep stairs and the cobbled streets run downhill through an oasis of terraced vineyards. At the top, the 18th century church stands next to the ruined fortifications that once protected a castle belonging to the counts of Cerdagne. The granite houses have tiled roofs and descend by stages into the valley, which shelters a beautiful Romanesque chapel.

Gruissan

South of Narbonne-Plage, Gruissan is built like a wreath around the rock that supports the tower of Barberousse. This fishing village borders on a marsh and a lake, connected to the sea by a channel. Its typically mediterranean houses huddle close to one another and have the particular charm of old Languedoc villages. A less attractive seaside resort has been constructed in the vicinity, partly on piles, as well as a port for pleasure boats.

The Vermilion Coast, between Argelès and Cerbère on the Spanish frontier, is as famous for its summer traffic jams as for the beauty of the scenery that it reveals. Between the Albères Massif and the Mediterranean Sea, ports and beaches line the jagged coastline. Collioure is one of the most beautiful. In the early 20th century it was a meeting place for many painters, among whom were Derain, Picasso and Foujita. The rose-colored dome of the church of Saint-Vincent, that looks out over the blue sea, as well as the old quarter of Mouré, still inspire artists and visitors. Around Banyuls, the hills are covered with vineyards that produce a sweet wine similar to the one from Rivesaltes, north of Perpignan.

Further north, in the Corbières region, scrubland alternates with vineyards throughout the Aude region, all the way to Narbonne. Here, a small village nestles, made famous by a story by Alphonse Daudet. Cucugnan is not in Provence but in the middle of Cathar country, between Quéribus and Peyrepertuse. The keep of Quéribus, protected by three lines of defensive walls, stands on a peak which offers a view of the Mediterranean, some nineteen miles away. Peyrepertuse was one of the most powerful fortresses in the area which, according to the vagaries of history, defended the north of the kingdom of Spain or the south of France, after it was bought by Saint Louis in the 13th century. Perched on a ridge in the Hautes-Corbières, the fortress forms a gigantic stone vessel from which the view is breathtaking. Numerous other equally spectacular Cathar sites are scattered across the region: for example, Puilaurens and the castle of Termes, whose fall was a decisive event in the crusade by Simon de Montfort.

Somewhat farther north, Lagrasse, on the contrary, supported the Catholic Party. An abbey was built there as early as the 8th century. A legend credits Charlemagne with its foundation, which is doubtful. It grew steadily until the 13th century. The village, which has extended to the other bank of the Orbieu, still has remnants of its ramparts from the 14th century, houses and a covered market from the same period. The alleys where many artisans now live are adorned by fountains, mullioned windows and carved beams decorating limestone houses roofed with tiles.

West of Carcassonne, Bram, a small medieval fortified village encircling its church, sheltered many Cathars. Simon de Montfort displayed a cruelty which he intended to be exemplary: he had the prisoners' eyes gouged out and their ears and noses cut off. The city of Carcassonne is a superb example of medieval architecture, crowned by its famous towers. Viollet-le-Duc has contributed a lot –too much according to some– to its restoration. This is also true of Narbonne, which has some beautiful vestiges around the Cathedral of Saint-Just.

A little to the south of Béziers, the Hérault region begins. During the Middle Ages, the castle in Minerve was the seat of the counts of the Minerve county, covered with vineyards, on the border of the Montagne Noire. The village stands at the confluence of two rivers on a dry spur, in a wild setting. It had to capitulate to the army of Simon de Montfort, who had succeeded in depriving it of water by destroying its only well. The sturdy houses, high and flat-roofed, are still dominated by the "candela," the keep of the old castle. The Romanesque church contains rare and precious vestiges from the 5th century.

In the heart of the Espinouse Mountains, La Salvetat-sur-Agout, although in the highlands, is surrounded by more gentle slopes. The village was created around a priory in the 11th century and still has remnants of the ramparts and old slate-covered houses, as does Fraisse, somewhat further along the Agout River.

Saint-Guilhem-le-Désert, east of Lodève, is, with good reason, one of the most visited villages in the region. A long line of ocher-colored houses with tiled roofs stretches between arid cliffs in the narrow gorges of the Verdus, a tiny tributary of the Hérault River. Formerly called Gellone, the village owes its present name to Guillaume the Great, Count of Narbonne, who first distinguished himself in war, in particular against the Saracens. In 804, delighted by the austere beauty and isolation of the site, he founded a Benedictine monastery he withdrew to a few years later to end his life in quiet contemplation. However, in a well-known *chanson de gestes* Guillaume d'Orange, modeled on the real Guillaume, is the grandson of Charles Martel and companion of Charlemagne. The popularity of its founder and the presence inside its walls of a relic of the true Cross, donated by the emperor, contribute to the fame of the abbey. After the troubles of the 10th century, it developed enormously, increasing its influence and its possessions while the village prospered.

Bram

This village in the Aude region lies halfway between Castelnaudary and Carcassonne. Its perfectly concentric layout and its narrow alleys, encircling the church, are due to its role as a fortified stronghold during the Middle Ages. This now so peaceful village in the Lauragais region was the scene of terrible battles in the 13th century during the darkest hours of the persecution of the Cathars.

The pilgrims of the Middle Ages stopped there on the road to Compostella. In the same period, between the 11th and 13th centuries, the monastery and, later, the village, was given the name of Guillaume.

In 1569, Saint-Guilhem was taken over by the Protestants. The abbey, already in decline because of the controversy over benefits, was deserted. At the end of the Wars of Religion, it was restored and recovered its influential position, which lasted until the Revolution, when the buildings were destroyed. Although the remnants of the monastery were included on the list of historical monuments as early as 1840, it was not until the middle of the 20th century that it was given serious attention. Saint-Guilhem then became a meeting point for those who love spectacular views and picturesque old villages. From the surrounding heights one can admire the terraces and tiled roofs layered on the slope beneath the church and its cloister. Along the narrow alleys and passages, the medieval houses combine the solidity, typical of Cévennes architecture, with the grace of the Renaissance: ornate capitals, mullioned windows and doors with carved lintels. The village was for a long time an important center of silkworm production.

The raising of silkworms was widespread in the Cévennes, as for example, in Saint-Jean-du-Gard, a lovely little village on the banks of the River Gardon. While the Aude region is alive with memories of the struggle between Cathars and crusaders, the region of the Cévennes was for a long time the scene of conflicts between the Catholics and the Camisards, the name given to the Cévennes Protestants. Even before the revocation of the Edict of Nantes, which prohibited the practice of their religion in 1685, the many Protestants in the region suffered persecution, which culminated in the terrible "dragoonings" organized by Louis XIV. The Protestant safe havens, established almost a century earlier, were hit particularly hard – Mas-Soubeyran and Mialet, for instance. One of the leaders of the Camisards was born near Alès, in Mas-Soubeyran, where a museum recounts this dark period in history. Mialet, nearby, still has its stalwart old houses, built on three levels, at a time when the inhabitants raised silkworms. The upper floor was reserved for them, the people lived underneath and the ground floor was occupied by the farm animals and stores.

Villefranche-de-Conflent

Contrary to most fortified villages in the Pyrénées, Villefranche is not situated on a height but in a confined valley whose entrance it defended from the 11th century on. The fortifications, strengthened in the 17th century by Vauban, shelter a group of beautiful medieval houses, near Saint-Martin-de-Canigou and Saint-Michel-de-Cuxa, the two major mystical sites in the region.

Following pages

Saint-Guilhem-le-Désert

This beautiful village near Lodève, like many others at the time, developed around an abbey, built in the 9th century. It owes its name to its founder, Guillaume the Great, Count of Narbonne. Saint-Guilhem was formerly a center of silkworm farming. Today, artists and artisans inhabit the ocher-colored houses in a maze of stone and vegetation, surrounded by magnificent scenery.

In his youth, Racine stayed in Uzès in the Garrigues. As he was an orphan, he was entrusted to a relation who was a curate in order to try to wean him away from a career in the theater. Much later, the writer André Gide went there to spend his holidays with his paternal grandmother. Near Uzès, the Valley of the Cèze cradles many pretty villages, such as Lussan, where once wool and silk were spun.

Moving up toward the Auvergne region, one passes into the Lozère Cévennes, bordering to the west on the Grands Causses. These vast limestone plateaus where sheep graze also hide wonderful sites like the caves of Dargilan or the chasm of Armand with its fantastic limestone concretions. To the east, Mount Lozère rises up where the houses melt into the granite, which in some places creates astonishingly chaotic scenery. Although the Lozère region is the least populated in France, it is a beautiful country with lovely villages such as La Canourgue and Sainte-Enimie, built on the rugged slopes of the gorges of the River Tarn. On the banks of the Lot, Mende, the only large city in the region, has pretty, old streets in the area around its cathedral.

PROVENCE CÔTE D'AZUR

"Provence has seen, has accommodated all peoples. And they have not wanted to re-embark. The Greeks, the Spaniards, the Italians have preferred the hot figs of Fréjus to those of Ionia or Tusculum," wrote Michelet. A melting-pot where all the Mediterranean peoples have been mixed together, Provence has for centuries been nourished by their diversity. This province is by its history, its geography, its topography, its vegetation and its buildings much more complex than is generally believed. First of all, it is a rainbow of colors: the white of the stones in the houses and on the rocky outcrops, the red of the roof tiles, the blue of the sky, the silver of the olive trees, the yellow of the mimosa, the violet of the lavender. And then, the fragrances; those that the perfumers of Grasse turn into scent and those of the herbs that enliven the Provençal cuisine: thyme, rosemary and many others. Its name calls up a vision of hills baked by the sun, of villages vibrating to the song of the cicadas and the sound of the voices in a play by Pagnol. But it is also a country of mountains, the Alps, a mythical sea, the Mediterranean, edged with beaches and narrow inlets, and of the vast expanse of the Camargue. Here, the windows of the mansions, farmhouses and cottages are small so as to keep out the sun and the prevailing north wind, the mistral. They are built of dry stone or have an ocher-colored finish and roofs of Roman tiles. Cypress hedges are planted here and there in an attempt to divert the ferocious wind that is called "tramontane" when it crosses the border to the Languedoc region.

In all their variety, the Provençal landscapes have one feature in common, that of having been shaped by the climate and by the Mediterranean peoples. It is not without reason that the literature of the south was called Provençal in the 12th and 13th centuries. Then, everything that was subtle and gracious in the genius of the province came to the fore. But all of Provence "can be found in Mirabeau, the strength of the bull, the majesty of the Rhône," again according to Michelet.

Eze

In the heart of the Riviera, between Nice and Menton, this village stands 1,300 feet above the Mediterranean. A path leading down to the sea bears the name of Friedrich Nietzsche, who wrote part of Zarathustra *here. We owe these beautifully perched villages to the foresight of the original inhabitants, who built them where they could be protected from the pirates who pillaged the coasts.*

The court of the counts of Provence, and particularly that of King René, in the 15th century, was a place of exquisite refinement. From its time as the capital of Provence, Aix has preserved many beautiful mansions that are scattered along the streets and squares, waiting to be discovered on a leisurely walk around the city. Mirabeau represented "the city of a thousand fountains" in the general assembly of 1789. Vauvenargues and Paul Cézanne were born here and the latter spent his youth in Aix. When at school, he befriended a new boy, Emile Zola, and a lasting friendship and an invaluable correspondence ensued. Cézanne frequently returned to Provence, visiting the banks of the Arc and the Sainte-Victoire mountain. He has left famous paintings of both, and their red ocher colors are said to stem from the earth that he picked up from the hills to mix with his paints.

To the west, near Marseille and the coastal lake of Berre, lies the delta of the Rhône River whose alluvial deposits have created the vast plain of the Camargue. Herds of cattle and horses graze here, watched by their guardians among an astonishingly rich flora and fauna. Every year in May, the Saintes-Maries-de-la-Mer pilgrimage attracts large crowds, among them many gypsies who come to worship their patroness, Sara. Together with Mary Jacobe and Mary Salome, Sara is said to have been miraculously cast up on these shores after having drifted around in a boat without sail or oars. This event is commemorated by processions and religious ceremonies where the ancient costumes of the city of Arles are worn by many. Some distance to the east, the ridge of the Alpilles lifts its arid white crests above pine-covered limestone slopes.

Beyond Fontvieille and the writer Daudet's famous windmill, les Baux-de-Provence appears on a rocky spur. Today the village is almost deserted, but it was built beneath a great fortress, whose remaining ruins have an impressive, almost ghostlike appearance and a wonderful view. The site, forming a natural stronghold, was inhabited as early as the Neolithic Period and fortified in the Middle Ages by a powerful Provençal family. In the 11th century, the lords of Les Baux extended their dominion over a great number of surrounding cities, but their boundless ambition made the lives of their subjects anything but restful; battles and sieges succeeded each other into the 15th century. Then, Les Baux fell into the hands of King René, who created a celebrated court of love in the city. When Les Baux became the property of the king of France, life there finally grew more peaceful.

Beyond Beaucaire and Tarascon, two names that recall the stories by Daudet, one arrives in Avignon, of which the author writes in *Letters From My Windmill*: "If one has not seen Avignon at the time of the popes, one has seen nothing. Here sounded the clicking of the lace-makers' looms, the little hammers of the goldsmiths chasing communion vessels, the soundboards being fitted by the lute makers, the hymns sung by the women weaving: above it all, the ringing of the bells and always a few drummers that could be heard rumbling somewhere down by the bridge."

To the north of the Comtat Venaissin region, the alleys of Séguret, near the Dentelles de Montmirail Range, invite a pleasant walk among its old houses and fountains, as does Malaucène with its old church, at the foot of Mount Ventoux. This chalk mountain battered by the mistral was in Roman times a place of worship dedicated to the god of the winds. The barren beauty of the site delighted Petrarch, who climbed up to its 650 feet summit.

In the 19th century, the entomologist Fabre spent his entire life studying the extremely varied flora and fauna on its slopes. The wonderful panorama from the top of the Ventoux recalls some lines from a story by Daudet, "The Stars": "If you have ever spent a night under the stars, you know that while we sleep a mysterious world awakes in the silence and the solitude. All the spirits of the mountain come and go freely." As the seasons follow each other, the country around the mountain lives according to a centuries-old rhythm: the moving of the sheep in the spring, the violet rows of the lavender fields in the summer, the grape harvest on the slopes of Mount Ventoux in the fall and the gathering of the olives in the winter. The villages of Brantes, Bédoin and Flassan have built their ocher-colored stone houses, their church towers, their small shady squares in the foothills.

To the north of the Albion Plateau, Montbrun-les-Bains, although it belongs to the Drôme region, has all the characteristics of a provençal village. From the crown of a hill, dominated by the ruins of a castle, its houses descend to a plain dotted with cypresses. In the 16th century, the lord of Montbrun, a staunch Protestant, was executed for having wrought vengeance on the Catholics after the massacre of Saint-Bartholomew. Today Montbrun is a green oasis in this arid landscape.

The Lubéron is a mixture of forests and rocky outcrops where myriad villages are perched on rocky

Roussillon

North of the Lubéron region, Roussillon overlooks the Valley of the Fairies, surrounded by the ocher quarries that have made it famous. All the shades of ocher, from pale yellow to red, color the houses of the compact little village. Vaulted passages and steep alleys invite the visitor to escape the blistering provençal sun by a leisurely walk in their shade.

spurs above a landscape where pines, hackberry trees, cedars and olive trees grow side by side with thyme, rosemary and lavender. The pinkish stone of the houses, the winding streets and vaulted passages, the fragrances in the air, together compose, between sun and shade, a quintessential picture of Provence; good

examples are Oppède-le-Vieux, Lourmarin, Ansouis and Lacoste, whose lord was the Marquis de Sade. In Ménerbe, stretching out along its high plateau, beautiful houses and some magnificent mansions surround a fortress which was desperately fought over in the Wars of Religion. From the old church one has a view of Gordes, clinging to the edge of the Vaucluse Plateau. It stands on a cliff, around a medieval castle. The castle, remodeled in the 16th century, enchanted the painter Vasarely, who is honored by a museum there. A remnant of its old defensive walls, a paved walk, offers a view of the plain that spreads out at the foot of the cliff from Apt to Cavaillon and Mount Ventoux. In olden days, silkworm farmers and weavers populated the village, while olive trees and madder were grown all around it. The madder was used to produce a red dye.

South of Gordes lies the village of the "bories," small round, conical, rectangular or square huts built of dry stone which, depending on the period, served as places of safety, temporary shelters for shepherds and their flocks, or simply as storehouses. They exist throughout the south of France, but those in Gordes are curious in that they form a large farm. Inside a closed courtyard, each one has its own particular function: living quarters, bread oven or storage. A few miles away, one of the masterpieces of Cistercian art is to be found: the abbey of Sénanque. Petrarch lived quite some time in the area, near a marvel of nature, the resurgence of an underground river, La Fontaine-de-Vaucluse. He stayed because he could not bear to leave his impossible love, Laura, whose beauty he praised in many of his poems. Some distance farther east, the houses of Roussillon are painted in all possible shades of ocher, from yellow to red. The quarries from which it comes export a large proportion of their production.

The tiny village of Lure is situated between the valley of the Durance River and the arid mountain of Lure. Here, the bishops of Sisteron used to have their summer residence. At the time, it was a busy town alive with artisans and shepherds. Now, an international workshop on graphic art is held every summer among the beautiful corbelled houses and small shady squares of Lure. The novels by Jean Giono, born in Manosque, are permeated by the wild landscape around it: limestone rocks dotted with olive trees, thyme and lavender, scorched by the sun in summer and battered by the mistral at all times of the year.

Moustiers-Sainte-Marie was renowned for the manufacture of glazed earthenware in the 18th century. Antique pieces are exposed in a superb crypt arranged as a museum, and one can visit the stores and workshops where the tradition is carried on. Moustiers was founded by a colony of monks in the 5th century and the chapel Notre-Dame-de-Beauvoir watches over it from its cliff above the village. The path that leads up to it reveals the beauty of the scenery. A torrent cuts the cliff in half; a chain decorated with a star is said to have been stretched across it as an offering of thanksgiving by a knight returning from the Holy Land.

Simiane-la-Rotonde

The "rotunda" that crowns Simiane is a remnant of a castle from the 12th century. Today, it hosts a festival of ancient music every summer. Climbing up the sides of a hill, the streets are decorated with ornate doors, vaulted entrances and small windows whose shutters are closed to keep out the provençal sun. All around, the landscape of lavender and olive trees recalls the atmosphere of the novels by Giono.

Bridges spanning the torrent, which runs through the village, narrow streets and vaulted passages, whitewashed houses, a church with a spire pierced by twinned windows – Moustiers is an irresistibly charming, labyrinthine village linking the mineral wall to the gentle countryside.

After having been a winter resort for 19th century aristocrats, the Riviera has been disfigured in the 20th century by constructions of questionable quality, destined for teeming masses of tourists. Luckily the coast and, particularly the countryside inland, still have ports, beaches and villages of unquestionable beauty and charm.

The Corniche des Maures leads to Le Lavandou, a small port with a fragrant name, to the beautiful beach at Pampelonne, near Ramatuelle, where Gérard Philipe is buried, and Saint-Tropez, the haunt of Colette and Cocteau and any number of artists who assembled there in the Fifties.

Another corniche road runs through the Esterel massif, between Saint-Raphaël and Cannes. Pine forests cling to the sides of its rough, although not very high, ridges that plunge into the sea forming rocky points and narrow inlets. Around Juan-les-Pins and Antibes, the towns and villages on their mimosa-scented hilltops have been hosts to numerous painters. In Antibes, the Picasso museum shows work that he did in the surrounding area and the ceramics that he created in Vallauris. In the Photographic museum of Mougins, there are many portraits of Picasso and the friends who came to see him. At Cagnes-sur-Mer, the

the twenties: Signac, Soutine, Chagall and many others were among the guests. Its walls are covered with their paintings, interspersed with photographs of all the celebrities of literature and film who used to spend time here.

Further inland, the steep cobbled streets of Seillans enchanted Max Ernst, who stayed and painted there. It is as charming as every village perched on a hilltop, like Gattières and, farther east, Gourdon, which is a true eagle's nest, near the gorges of the Loup. Tourrette-sur-Loup, between Grasse and Vence, has specialized in growing violets. Attracted by its marvelous setting, artisans and artists have also settled in the fortified village. These rocky peaks were once appreciated for the protection that they offered against armed attacks; today it is their peace and quiet that attract the visitors.

In the country behind Nice, a multitude of villages hide all sorts of surprises. For example, Coaraze, which has a square decorated with sun dials designed by various artists, among them Cocteau. Lucéram where steep stairs and shady alleys, cooled by splashing fountains, climb ever upward. To gain space on the narrow rocky ledge that supports it, its inhabitants have often extended the first floor of their houses across the street by a bridgelike structure, called "ponti." Sospel stands on the banks of the river Bévéra; Peille is a medieval village on a hillside; Peillon rises above the rocks where a chapel of the White Penitents shelters its beautiful 15th century frescoes; Sainte-Agnès, at the foot of a rose-colored limestone cliff. All of these villages, although they are close to the coast, have been protected from the depredations of tourism.

Inland, toward the Italian border, the Mercantour Massif rises to a height of over 6,500 feet. A nature reserve protects the particularly rich mountain flora and fauna that flourish among the cirques, lakes and torrents. The valley of Les Merveilles, close to mount Bégo, hides many cave paintings, some dating from the Bronze Age. To the north, in the Queyras Mountains, stands the highest village in Europe, Saint-Véran, at an altitude of 6,500 feet. Its old mountain chalets are built of wood and have a gallery for storing hay and straw for the animals. Around it, the summer hiking trails become ski trails in the winter.

house where Renoir spent the last years of his life now shows some of his work. Saint-Paul, near Vence, is famous for its museum of modern art, the Maeght Foundation, established in a pink and white building on the hill of Les Gardettes. In the village, the inn La Colombe d'Or became a meeting point for painters in

Gordes

In the sturdy houses along the winding streets of Gordes, silkworms were bred in the old days. In the plain below, among the thyme and the rosemary, olives and madder were grown. In the 1960s, the medieval castle was made into a museum for the paintings of Vasarely, who lived and worked here. Remnants of the covered walk along the ruined ramparts offer a beautiful view of the plain that fans out at the foot of the village, from Apt to Cavaillon, and the Mount Ventoux.

CORSICA

Corsica, this fragment of mountain that emerges from the Mediterranean Sea and rises to a height of 8,800 feet in its northern reaches, offers fantastic views of mountains, cut by deep valleys and gently sloping toward the south and the east. Winding roads clinging to the mountain sides, maquis, vineyards, olive groves, pine forests, a coast deeply indented by inlets lined with fine sand, villages that seem suspended in thin air; "the island of beauty" could not have found a better name for itself.

Very early, the island had many suitors. The Phoenicians established trading posts here, then came the Etruscans, followed by the Cathaginians before the Romans settled here. At the beginning of our era, Rome exiled certain undesirable elements to Corsica – for example, Seneca. After having experienced a long series of invasions, the island became the property of Pisa in the 11th century. Pisa was, however, obliged to share sovereignty with Genoa, which, in 1284, obtained total sovereignty over the island. The Genovese rule lasted for almost five centuries in spite of numerous conflicts. Venice, Aragon and France laid claim to Corsica who, itself, desired independence, and this led to incessant turmoil until the 16th century. In 1557, Corsica was integrated into the kingdom of France, but reverted to Genoa two years later. After a period of relative peace marked by memories of the centuries of struggle, the island again erupted into war in the 18th century. The War of Independence set Genoa, France and the Corsicans against each other. In 1735, the Corsicans proclaimed their independence under the direction of a triumvirate. France continued to pursue its conquest until, in 1768, Genoa finally relinquished the island to the French. In spite of strong resistance under the leadership of Pascal Paoli, Corsica adopted the status of French administrative region in 1790. Paoli, having allied himself with the English, came back from exile to try to obtain independence. The "Anglo-Corsican" kingdom that ensued was, in reality, subject to English rule. The hopes of independence were once again disappointed and France regained its sovereignty over the island. In the meantime, Bonaparte, who missed by one year being born Italian,

started his brilliant career. The strife did not end, however, and a number of insurrections followed each other until the 19th century. Even today, separatist movements continue to claim independence. In 1975, Corsica was divided into two administrative units, Haute-Corse and Corse-du-Sud. In 1982 it obtained the special status of a partially autonomous territory.

Cape Corse, in the north, has, to the west, a series of rugged formations that plunge into the sea; to the east, the coastline is lower and straighter.

Piana

This picture of the village shows it serenely nestling between the fragrant green hills and the blue sea, but Piana is particularly well known for the beauty of its narrow inlets in the coast below. In spite of their beauty, a diabolic legend is attached to them. Satan, in love with a shepherdess who repulsed his amorous advances with the help of her husband, became so enraged that he created a mass of gigantic rocks, imprisoning the woman, her husband and their dog. Saint Martin, hearing the noise, arrived and started to pray for the unfortunates: his prayers were heard by the heavens and a huge wave rolled in and became the Gulf of Porto.

Centuri-Port shelters its softly colored fishermen's houses in a cove on the western coast. Farther to the south, Nonza crowns a rocky spur with dizzying slopes. The church is dedicated to Saint Julie, the patron saint of Corsica, who was born in Nonza. A ruined Genovese tower watches over the village; such towers, reminders of the frequent invasions, are scattered all along the Corsican coastline.

South of the cape, in Saint-Florent, stands a Genovese citadel from the 15th century. The small port at the head of the gulf, surrounded by mountains, boasts one of the most beautiful Romanesque churches in the Pisan style. On the opposite coast, on the Tyrrhenian Sea, the houses in Erbalunga huddle at the edge of the sea, their feet almost in the water.

South of Cap Corse, Bastia, the largest city on the island, still has the charm of the old port, surrounded by the quarter of "Terra-Vecchia," from which it grew into the city of today.

The rocky hills of the Agriates region were formerly farmed by the inhabitants of Cap Corse. The dry-stone huts, that were used to store grain and later to shelter shepherds, were built during this period. Now it has been invaded by the maquis, the "desert," as Pierre Benoit calls it in his novel *The desert of Agrigates*, and is criss-crossed by paths in a landscape that recalls the Corsica of Mérimée's *Colomba*.

Ever since the Middle Ages, the Balagne region has been fertile and prosperous. The port city of L'Ile-Rousse was created in the 18th century by Pascal Paoli. The square named after him, shaded by plane trees, now lies in the heart of a popular summer resort.

Algajola still has its fortifications and its citadel, as does Calvi with its long and rich history. On the long beach lined with pine trees and in the harbor sheltered by its magnificent bay, summer visitors and pleasure craft have replaced the lobster fishermen and their boats.

streets and so do Cateri and Feliceto. In the mountainous heart of the island, Ghisoni lies hidden along the bottom of an almost inaccessible valley in the shadow of Kyrie Eleison and Christi Eleison, two rocks steeped in legend. Somewhat to the south, on the slopes of Mount Renoso, occupied by skiers in the winter, sheepfolds remind us that cheeses made from sheep and goat milk – for example, the famous Brocciu – are the pride of the Corsican table. Aléria, on the east coast, was the capital of the Roman province after having been first Phoenician, then Carthaginian. It has important vestiges from antiquity.

In southern Corsica, the wide gulf of Porto-Vecchio is surrounded by archeological sites, such as those at Arraggio and Torre. Farther inland, the Roman city of Cucuruzzu stands at the edge of the forest of Bavella, on the hill slopes below the needles of Bavella. The villages of Quenza and Zonza with their stalwart mountain houses stand out against the backdrop of these strangely shaped granite rocks that rise to a height of 5,200 feet. In the extreme south, the cliffs of Bonifacio face the coast of Sardinia. The old town, protected by a fortress, huddles around narrow streets where the houses are decorated with coats of arms, flanked by stairs without handrails (in the Corsican tradition) and sheltered from the sun by brightly colored shutters. Sartène with its labyrinth of vaulted passages has the same medieval character. The region has a wealth of megaliths, for example the menhirs at Pallaggiu, which number around a hundred. But the foremost prehistoric site on the island is Filitosa where dolmens and menhirs are mixed with stone sculptures of human figures. This region is also the cradle of Corsican wine, grown here before our era, between Propriano and Cargèse.

Ajaccio, of course, recalls Bonaparte, whose life and adventures are told in the house where he was born and in the Napoleonic Museum. The red porphyry of the Sanguinaires Islands appears off the point of Parata. Farther away, the same stone forms Capo Rosso, on the gulf of Porto, which has been named an international heritage site by UNESCO. Near Piana, the shore bristles with red- and rose-colored needles shaped by erosion. They are called "calanche" and they create one of the most magnificent sceneries on the island, overlooked by the picturesque village of Piana and its church with a Genovese belltower.

Away from the coast, the Balagne region is full of villages clinging to the hillsides. One of the most remarkable is Sant'Antonino. The granite houses and the cliffs melt into each other along the narrow cobbled streets that sometimes turn into steps, carved out of the rock, or vaulted passages under the houses. As is often the case in these perched villages that cannot grow laterally, the houses are very high because they have been extended upwards as the need for space has increased. Spelocato, nearby, has the same picturesque narrow

Lumio

In the heart of the high hill country, Lumio stands above the gulf of Calvi, capital of the Balagne region in the north, nicknamed "the garden of Corsica." Surrounded by olive groves, the village enjoys magnificent views of Mount Cinto, a few miles away; this is the highest summit on the island, rising to a lofty 8,800 feet. Some discern in the name of the village the Latin word for light – lumen – which would support the assumption that a temple dedicated to Apollo, the god of sun and light, lies beneath the small Romanesque church of San Pietro and San Paolo, located near the village.

Walnut harvest in the Corrèze region.

OLDEN TIMES IN FRENCH VILLAGES

Billom. S.t Cernin. Billy. Gannat. Cempde. Montferrand. Cesse.

Volvic. Vic sur cire. Lezoux. Latour. Aigueperse. Murat. Riaines.

Pont Gibaud. Issoire. S.t Martin. Mont dore. Riom. S.t Bonnet. S.t Chamand.

Tiesac. Polignac. Maurs. Thiers. Chergue. Aurillac. au Puy.

Mauriac. Ebreuil. Saugues. Issingeaux. Monistro. S.t Flour. Espaly.

S.t Simon. Plaux. Maringues. au Puy. Randan. Pierrefort. Ris.

114

Darjou A. Leroux.

123

Stone huts in Breuil, in Dordogne region.

One of the first plans for a farm, in the Somme, 1455.

LES ROUTES EXACTES DES PO[STES]

Le Nombre des Lieux qu'il y a de Paris aux Principales les Villes du Royaume etc.

DE PARIS A	Lieues
Abbeville	38
AIX en Pr.	‡ 150
Alais	‡ 140
Albi	‡ 140
Alencon	38
Alet	‡ 158
Amboise	57
Ambrun	140
Amiens	28
Amsterdam	
Angers	‡ 64
Angoulesme	110
Apt	145
Augsbourg	‡
Arras	‡ 40
Argentan	40
Arles	‡ 145
Arlon	78
Arnay le Duc	65
Avignon	‡ 138
Avranches	‡ 62
Aurilhac	112
Auch	‡ 145
Autun	65
Auxerre	‡ 40
Auxonne	72
Ayre	‡ 48
Bappaumes	34
Barbezieux	96
Bar le Duc	58
Barraux	120
Bar sur Aube	42
Bar sur Seine	30
Basle	106
Bastogne	85
Bayeux	62
Bayonne	‡ 142
Bazas	124
Beaucaire	144
Beaune	72
Beauvais	16
Befort	120
Belley	112
Belle Isle	106
Berg St. Winox	56
BERLIN	
BESANCON	‡ 82
Bethune	45
Beziers	160
Bich	95
Blanc	65
Blavet	140
Blaye	106
Blois	‡ 46
Bouchain	40
Bouillon	56
Boulogne	‡ 52
BOURDEAUX	110
Bourg	92
BOURGES	‡ 52
Brest	120
Briancon	140
Brie C. Robert	6
Briude	92
Brisach	108
Brouage	106
BRUSELLE	50
Caen	56
Cahors	‡ 118
Calais	60
Cambray	‡ 37
Carcassone	‡ 158
Carentan	72
Castres	‡ 150
Caudebec	34
Chaalons	39
Challon	78
Chambor	45
Charlemont	52
Chartres	‡ 19
Ch. Roux	62
Ch. Thierry	22
Chastelleraud	78
Chaumonten B.	50
Cherbourg	84
Cisteron	‡ 140
CLERMONT	‡ 80
Collioure	180
Colmar	104
COLOGNE	90
Compiegne	17
Condom	‡ 135
Cornuaille	‡ 128
Coutance	‡ 76
Crepy	13
Dammartin	8
Dax	‡ 132
Die	‡ 125
Dieppe	40
Digne	‡ 128
Dijon	66
Dole	75

DE PARIS A	Lieues
Douay	44
Dourlens	35
DRESDEN	
Dreux	‡ 16
Dunkerke	60
Dusseldorp	
Elna	‡ 176
Epernay	32
Estampes	13
Evreux	‡ 19
Falaise	44
Fescamp	48
la Fleche	54
Foix	‡ 152
Fontaine Bleau	14
Francfort	
Frejuls	‡ 169
Fribourg	112
GAND	‡ 65
Gap	‡ 140
GENEVE	‡ 105
Gex	‡ 104
Glandeves	‡ 170
Grace	‡ 172
Granville	68
Gravelines	58
Gray	74
GRENOBLE	‡ 118
Gueret	80
Guise	34
Ham	26
Hambourg	
HANOVER	
Harfleur	43
Havre de Grace	45
HEIDELBERG	
Hesdin	42
Hombourg	90
Honfleur	40
Huningue	112
Lonqui	33
Ipres	‡ 55
Issoire	86
Lssoudun	49
Laudau	105
Landrecy	40
Langres	‡ 57
Laon	29
Lavaur	‡ 136
Lectour	‡ 136
Leipsiek	
Liege	‡ 72
Lille	50
Limoges	‡ 83
Lisieux	‡ 34
Loches	64
Lodeve	‡ 132
Lombez	‡ 146
LONDRES	‡ 92
Longwye	68
Loudun	78

Pour la Commodité et la Sureté des Voyageurs, car celuy qui demande beaucoup s'egare le plus souvent et se retarde. aux depens TOB. CONR. LOTTER, Geogr. a Augsbourg.